Teaching with Manipulatives

Geometry

Glencoe

Manipulatives

Glencoe offers three types of kits to enhance the use of manipulatives in your Geometry classroom.

- The **Glencoe Mathematics Overhead Manipulative Resources** contains translucent manipulatives designed for use with an overhead projector.

- The **Glencoe Mathematics Classroom Manipulative Kit** contains classroom sets of frequently used manipulatives in algebra, geometry, measurement, probability, and statistics.

- The **Glencoe Mathematics Student Manipulative Kit** contains an individual set of manipulatives often used in Student Edition activities.

The manipulatives contained in each of these kits are listed on page vi of this booklet.

Each of these kits can be ordered from Glencoe by calling (800) 334-7344.

	ISBN	MHID
Glencoe Mathematics Overhead Manipulative Resources	978-0-07-830593-1	0-07-830593-4
Glencoe Mathematics Classroom Manipulative Kit	978-0-02-833116-4	0-02-833116-8
Glencoe Mathematics Student Manipulative Kit	978-0-02-833654-1	0-02-833654-2

Glencoe

The *McGraw·Hill* Companies

Send all inquiries to:
Glencoe/McGraw-Hill
8787 Orion Place
Columbus, OH 43240-4027

ISBN: 978-0-07-890524-7
MHID: 0-07-890524-9

Teaching Geometry with Manipulatives

Printed in the United States of America.

7 8 9 10 RHR 15 14 13

Contents

Teacher's Guide to Using
Teaching Geometry with Manipulatives

The book contains two sections of masters—Easy-to-Make Manipulatives and Geometry Labs. Tabs help you locate the chapter resources in each section. A complete list of manipulatives available in each of the three types of Glencoe Mathematics Manipulative Kits appears on the next page.

Easy-to-Make Manipulatives
The first section of this book contains masters for making your own manipulatives. To make more durable manipulatives, consider using card stock.

You can also make transparencies of frequently used items such as grid paper and number lines.

Activity Masters
Each chapter begins with **Teaching Notes and** Overview that summarizes the activities for the chapter and includes sample answers. There are four types of masters.

Mini-Projects are short projects that enable students to work cooperatively in small groups to investigate mathematical concepts.

Using Overhead Manipulatives provides instructions for the teacher to demonstrate an alternate approach to the concepts of the lesson by using manipulatives on the overhead projector.

Student Recording Sheets accompany the Geometry Labs found in the Student Edition. Students can easily record the results of the activity on prepared grids, charts, and figures.

Geometry Labs provide additional activities to enrich the students' experiences. These masters often include a transparency master to accompany the activity.

Glencoe Mathematics Manipulatives

Glencoe Mathematics Overhead Manipulative Resources
MHID: 0-07-830593-4
ISBN: 978-0-07-830593-1

Transparencies		Overhead Manipulatives
integer mat	centimeter grid	algebra tiles
equation mat	number lines	spinners
product mat	lined paper	two-dimensional cups
inequality mat	regular polygons	red and yellow counters
dot paper	polynomial models	decimal models (base-ten blocks)
isometric dot paper	integer models	compass
coordinate grids	equation models	protractor
		geoboard/geobands
		geometric shapes
		transparency pens in 4 colors

Glencoe Mathematics Classroom Manipulative Kit
MHID: 0-02-833116-8
ISBN: 978-0-02-833116-4

Algebra	Measurement, Probability, and Statistics	Geometry
algebra tiles	base-ten models	compasses
counters	marbles	geoboards
cups	measuring cups	geobands
centimeter cubes	number cubes	geomirrors
equation mat/product mat	protractors	isometric dot grid tamp
coordinate grid stamp and	rulers	pattern blocks
ink pad	scissors	pattern blocks
	spinners	tangrams
	stopwatches	
	tape measures	

Glencoe Mathematics Student Manipulative Kit
MHID: 0-02-833654-2
ISBN: 978-0-02-833654-1

algebra tiles	protractor
red and yellow counters	scissors
cups	geoboard
equation /product mat	geobands
compass/ruler	tape measure

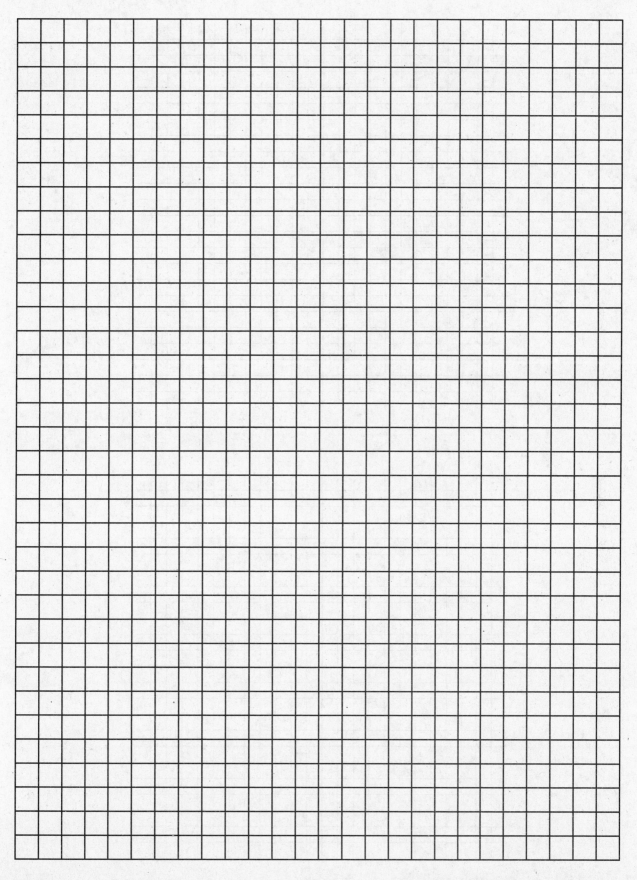

Teaching Geometry with Manipulatives

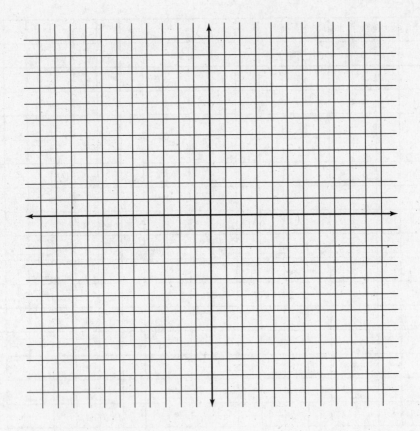

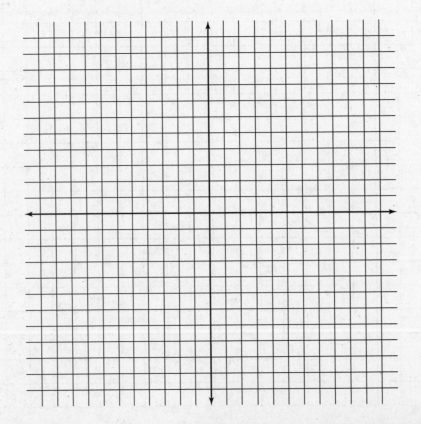

Teaching Geometry with Manipulatives

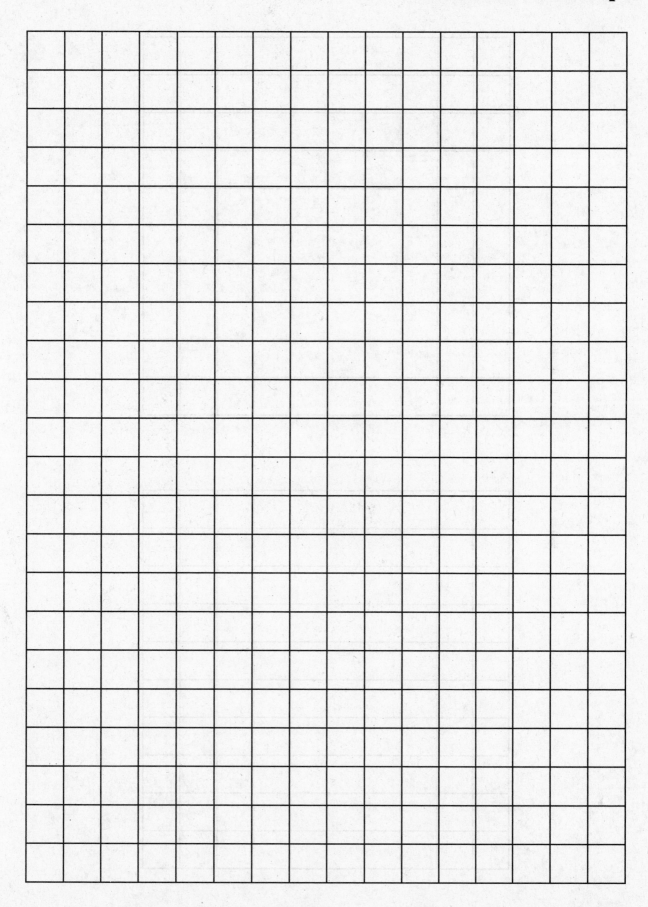

Teaching Geometry with Manipulatives

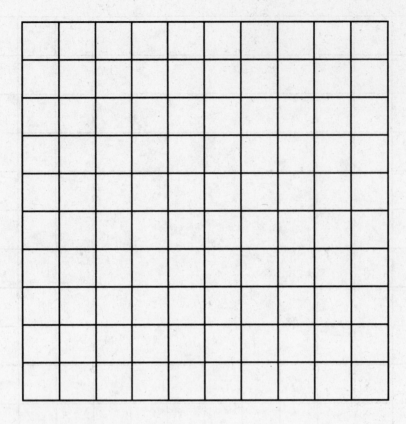

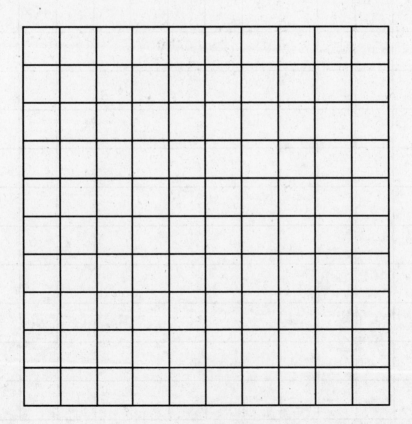

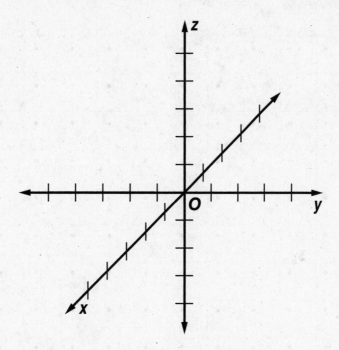

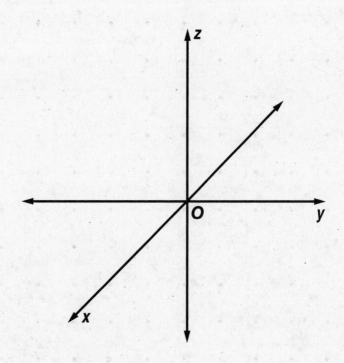

Teaching Geometry with Manipulatives

Teaching Geometry with Manipulatives

Two-Column Proof Format

Given:

Figure

Prove:

Plan:

Proof:

STATEMENTS	REASONS

Teaching Geometry with Manipulatives

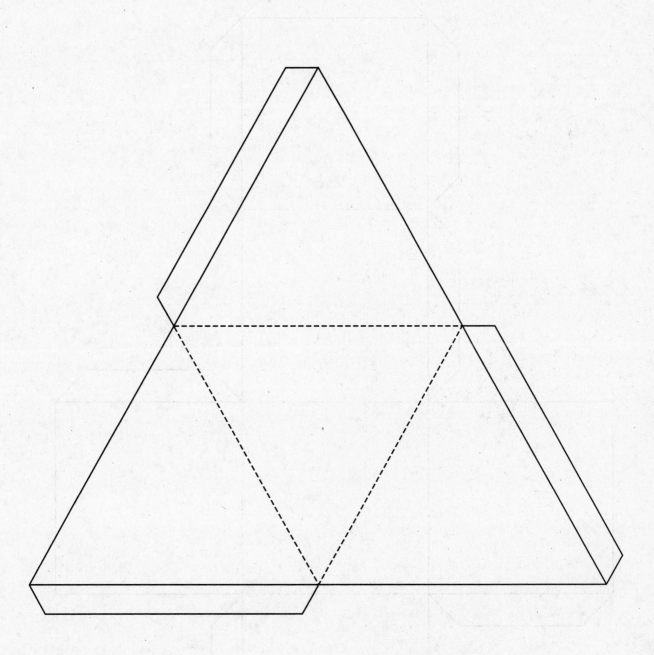

Teaching Geometry with Manipulatives

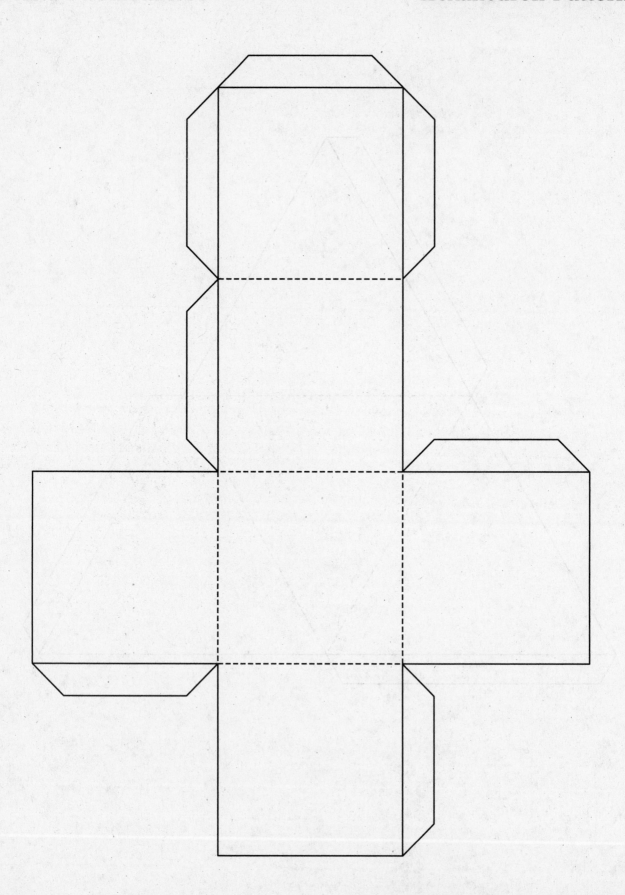

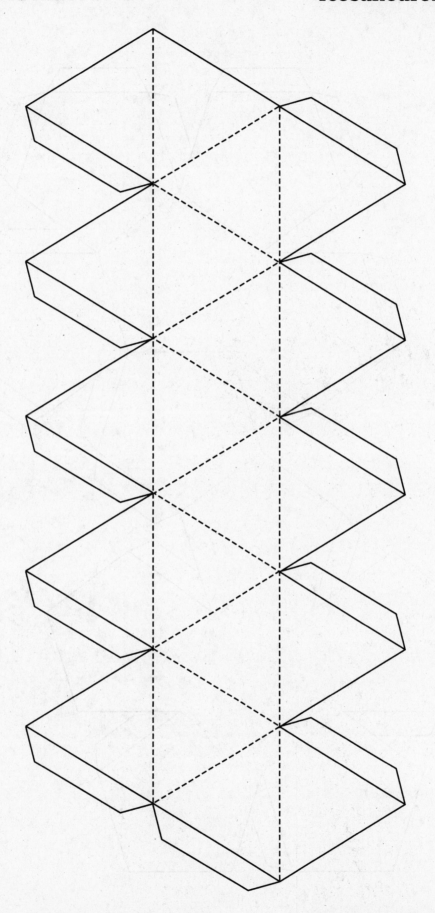

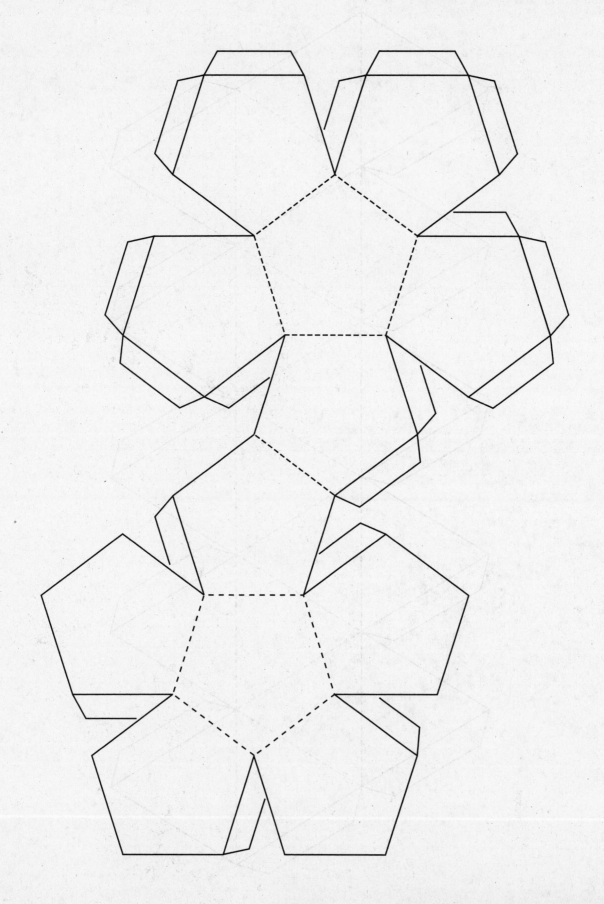

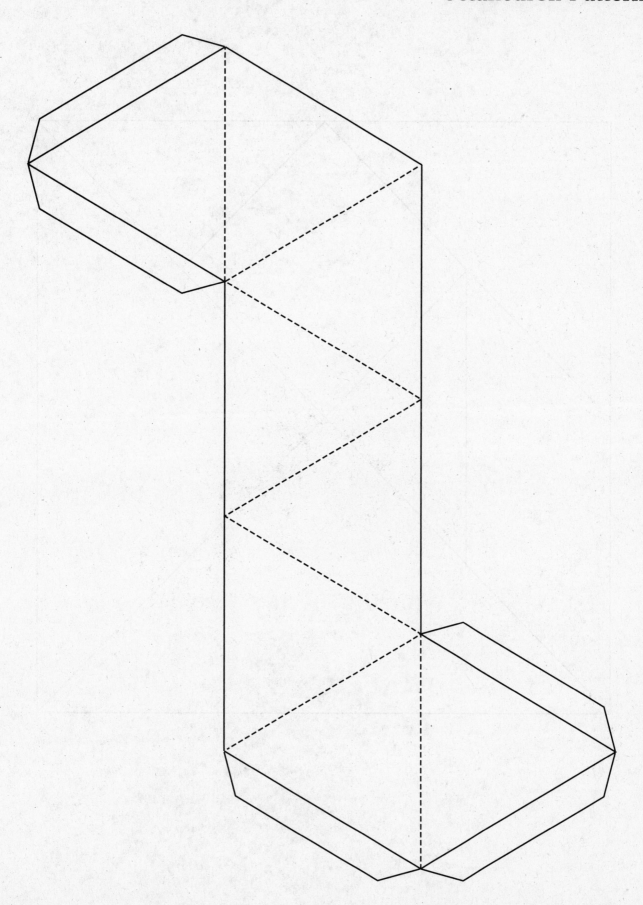

Teaching Geometry with Manipulatives

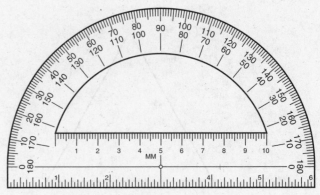

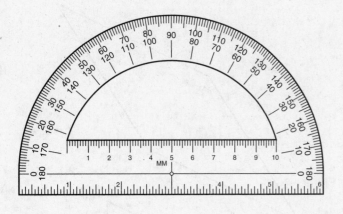

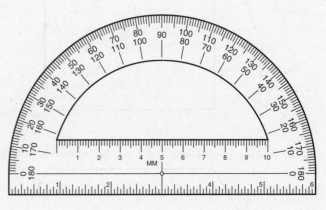

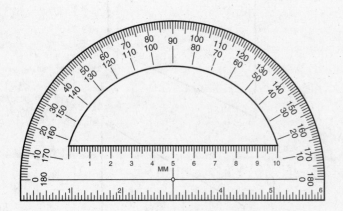

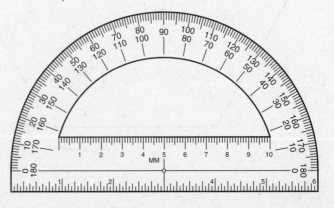

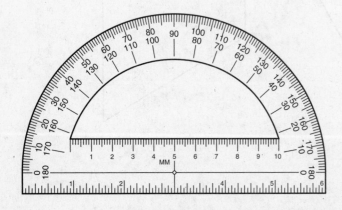

Teaching Geometry with Manipulatives

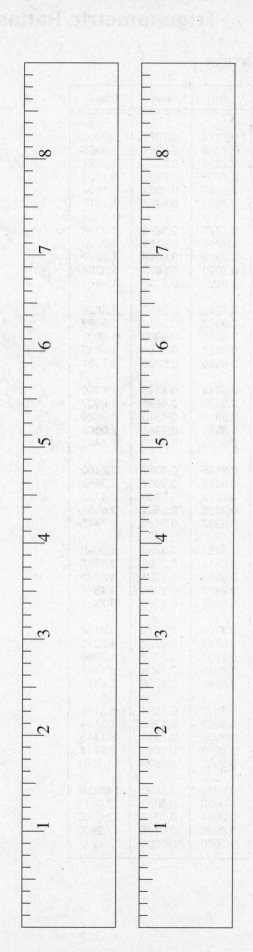

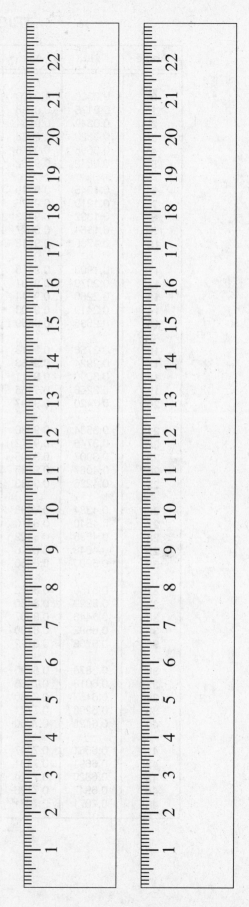

Teaching Geometry with Manipulatives

Trigonometric Ratios

TRIGONOMETRIC RATIOS

Angle	sin	cos	tan	Angle	sin	cos	tan
0°	0.0000	1.0000	0.0000	45°	0.7071	0.7071	1.0000
1°	0.0175	0.9998	0.0175	46°	0.7193	0.6947	1.0355
2°	0.0349	0.9994	0.0349	47°	0.7314	0.6820	1.0724
3°	0.0523	0.9986	0.0524	48°	0.7431	0.6691	1.1106
4°	0.0698	0.9976	0.0699	49°	0.7547	0.6561	1.1504
5°	0.0872	0.9962	0.0875	50°	0.7660	0.6428	1.1918
6°	0.1045	0.9945	0.1051	51°	0.7771	0.6293	1.2349
7°	0.1219	0.9925	0.1228	52°	0.7880	0.6157	1.2799
8°	0.1392	0.9903	0.1405	53°	0.7986	0.6018	1.3270
9°	0.1564	0.9877	0.1584	54°	0.8090	0.5878	1.3764
10°	0.1736	0.9848	0.1763	55°	0.8192	0.5736	1.4281
11°	0.1908	0.9816	0.1944	56°	0.8290	0.5592	1.4826
12°	0.2079	0.9781	0.2126	57°	0.8387	0.5446	1.5399
13°	0.2250	0.9744	0.2309	58°	0.8480	0.5299	1.6003
14°	0.2419	0.9703	0.2493	59°	0.8572	0.5150	1.6643
15°	0.2588	0.9659	0.2679	60°	0.8660	0.5000	1.7321
16°	0.2756	0.9613	0.2867	61°	0.8746	0.4848	1.8040
17°	0.2924	0.9563	0.3057	62°	0.8829	0.4695	1.8807
18°	0.3090	0.9511	0.3249	63°	0.8910	0.4540	1.9626
19°	0.3256	0.9455	0.3443	64°	0.8988	0.4384	2.0503
20°	0.3420	0.9397	0.3640	65°	0.9063	0.4226	2.1445
21°	0.3584	0.9336	0.3839	66°	0.9135	0.4067	2.2460
22°	0.3746	0.9272	0.4040	67°	0.9205	0.3907	2.3559
23°	0.3907	0.9205	0.4245	68°	0.9272	0.3746	2.4751
24°	0.4067	0.9135	0.4452	69°	0.9336	0.3584	2.6051
25°	0.4226	0.9063	0.4663	70°	0.9397	0.3420	2.7475
26°	0.4384	0.8988	0.4877	71°	0.9455	0.3256	2.9042
27°	0.4540	0.8910	0.5095	72°	0.9511	0.3090	3.0777
28°	0.4695	0.8829	0.5317	73°	0.9563	0.2924	3.2709
29°	0.4848	0.8746	0.5543	74°	0.9613	0.2756	3.4874
30°	0.5000	0.8660	0.5774	75°	0.9659	0.2588	3.7321
31°	0.5150	0.8572	0.6009	76°	0.9703	0.2419	4.0108
32°	0.5299	0.8480	0.6249	77°	0.9744	0.2250	4.3315
33°	0.5446	0.8387	0.6494	78°	0.9781	0.2079	4.7046
34°	0.5592	0.8290	0.6745	79°	0.9816	0.1908	5.1446
35°	0.5736	0.8192	0.7002	80°	0.9848	0.1736	5.6713
36°	0.5878	0.8090	0.7265	81°	0.9877	0.1564	6.3138
37°	0.6018	0.7986	0.7536	82°	0.9903	0.1392	7.1154
38°	0.6157	0.7880	0.7813	83°	0.9925	0.1219	8.1443
39°	0.6293	0.7771	0.8098	84°	0.9945	0.1045	9.5144
40°	0.6428	0.7660	0.8391	85°	0.9962	0.0872	11.4301
41°	0.6561	0.7547	0.8693	86°	0.9976	0.0698	14.3007
42°	0.6691	0.7431	0.9004	87°	0.9986	0.0523	19.0811
43°	0.6820	0.7314	0.9325	88°	0.9994	0.0349	28.6363
44°	0.6947	0.7193	0.9657	89°	0.9998	0.0175	57.2900
45°	0.7071	0.7071	1.0000	90°	1.0000	0.0000	∞

Teaching Geometry with Manipulatives

Problem:

Understand

Plan

Solve

Check

These steps
can help
you solve
problems.

CHAPTER 1

Tools of Geometry
Teaching Notes and Overview

 ## Mini-Project

Intersecting Planes
(p. 25 of this booklet)

Use With Lesson 1-1.

Objective Model the intersection of three planes.

Materials
four sheets of heavy construction paper
scissors*
* = available in Overhead Manipulative Resources

Students should work in groups of two or three for this activity. They are to use two of the pieces of construction paper to complete Steps 1–4 to illustrate the intersection of three planes. The students are guided to the conclusion that the intersection of three planes is a point.

Answers

1. $\overleftrightarrow{PR}$

2. $\overleftrightarrow{RS}$

3. $\overleftrightarrow{QR}$

4. point R; a point

5. See students' work.

6. Folded plane A sits straight with respect to plane B, but folded plane D slants with respect to plane C.

 ## Geometry Lab Recording Sheet

Describing What You See
(p. 26 of this booklet)

Use With Extend 1-1. This corresponds to the activity on page 13 in the Student Edition.

Objective Visualize and write about points, lines, and planes.

Materials
straightedge

Students will learn to describe points, lines, and planes using common geometric terms.

Answers
See Teacher Edition p. 13.

 ## Using Overhead Manipulatives

Bisecting a Segment
(p. 27 of this booklet)

Use With Lesson 1-3.

Objective Bisect a line segment.

Materials
straightedge
transparency pens*
compass*
blank transparency
* = available in Overhead Manipulative Resources

This demonstration involves using a compass and a straightedge to construct a segment bisector on a blank transparency. You may wish to have students complete the construction at their desks while you complete the construction on the overhead. Ask students for suggestions of different ways you may be able to complete the construction.

Answers
Answers appear on the teacher demonstration instructions on page 27.

Geometry Lab

Pythagorean Puzzle
(pp. 28–30 of this booklet)

Use With Lesson 1-3.

Objective Use a puzzle to discover the Pythagorean Theorem.

Materials
classroom set of Geometry Lab
worksheets
scissors*
blank transparency
* = available in Overhead Manipulative Resources

For this activity, students can work in pairs. Have students cut out the shapes on the worksheet. Instruct students to label the back of each shape with the title of the shape. Have students work with their partner to complete the activity. As you review the answers, select a student to form each of the four puzzles on the overhead. Discuss with students how their conjecture in Exercise 11 is a representation of the Pythagorean Theorem.

Answers

1.

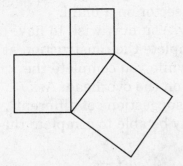

2. The length of a side of square A is equal to the length of one leg of the right triangle. The length of a side of square B is equal to the length of one leg of the right triangle. The length of a side of square C is equal to the length of the hypotenuse.

3.

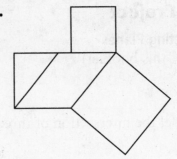

4. They are equal.

5.

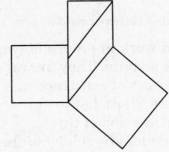

6. They are equal.

7.

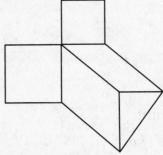

8. They are equal.

9. area of parallelogram B; area of parallelogram A; area of square C

10. area of square A + area of square B = area of square C

11. The area of the square on one leg plus the area of the square on the other leg is equal to the area of the square on the hypotenuse.

Using Overhead Manipulatives

Measuring Angles
(p. 31 of this booklet)

Use With Lesson 1–4.

Objective Measure angles by using a protractor.

Materials
protractor*
transparency pens*
transparency prepared as described below
* = available in Overhead Manipulative Resources

This demonstration involves using a protractor to measure an angle. You may wish to draw several angles of different measures on blank transparencies. Then ask students to come to the overhead and use a protractor to measure each angle.

In the extension, students are asked to use a protractor to draw an angle that measures 125°. You may wish to first demonstrate on the overhead how to use a protractor to draw an angle of a given measure other than 125°.

Answers
Answers appear on the teacher demonstration instructions on page 31.

Using Overhead Manipulatives

Constructing Congruent Angles
(p. 32 of this booklet)

Use With Lesson 1-4.

Objective Construct an angle congruent to a given angle.

Materials
transparency pens*
compass*
straightedge
protractor*
blank transparency
* = available in Overhead Manipulative Resources

This demonstration involves using a compass and straightedge to construct an angle congruent to a given angle. You may wish to review with students how to use a compass. Remind students that it is important to keep the same compass setting in order for the angles to be congruent. The protractor is used as a way to check your construction. Measure each angle with the protractor to verify that they are congruent.

Answers
Answers appear on the teacher demonstration instructions on page 32.

Using Overhead Manipulatives

Constructing Angle Bisectors
(p. 33 of this booklet)

Use With Lesson 1-4.

Objective Construct the bisector of a given angle.

Materials
transparency pens*
compass*
straightedge
protractor*
blank transparency
* = available in Overhead Manipulative Resources

This demonstration involves using a compass and straightedge to bisect an angle. You may wish to have students complete the construction at their desks while you complete the construction on the overhead. Have students draw any size angle to bisect. They can perform the same steps that you do at the overhead. Have students use a protractor to measure each half of the bisected angle to make sure they performed the construction correctly.

This extension involves using a straightedge and compass to construct an angle that is twice the size of a given angle. After you complete the construction at the overhead, you may wish to have students complete the construction at their desks with any angle they draw.

Answers
Answers appear on the teacher demonstration instructions on page 33.

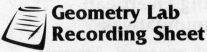

Geometry Lab Recording Sheet
Constructing Perpendiculars
(p. 34 of this booklet)

Use With Extend 1-5. This corresponds to the activity on page 55 in the Student Edition.

Objective Construct a line perpendicular to a given line through a

point on the line and through a point not on the line.

Materials
compass*
straightedge
* = available in Overhead Manipulative Resources

As a follow-up to Lesson 1-5, students construct perpendicular lines, both through a point on the line and a point not on the line. You may wish to demonstrate each construction at the overhead first. Then have students use the recording sheet to construct the perpendicular lines on their own. Once students have completed the activity, discuss how the two constructions are similar and different.

Answers
See Teacher Edition page 55.

Geometry Lab Recording Sheet
Orthographic Drawings and Nets
(pp. 35–36 of this booklet)

Use With Extend 1-7. This corresponds to the activity on page 75 in the Student Edition.

Objective Make a model of a three-dimensional solid given an orthographic drawing or net.

Materials
blocks
large sheet of paper
ruler
scissors
tape
isometric dot paper

Answers
See Teacher Edition p. 75.

NAME _____ DATE _____ PERIOD _____

Mini-Project

(Use with Lesson 1-1)

Intersecting Planes

In order to visualize the intersection of three planes, make a model. Use four sheets of heavy construction paper and scissors.

Step 1: Label the four sheets plane A, plane B, plane C, and plane D.

Step 2: Fold plane A in half to form planes A_1 and A_2.

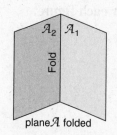

plane A folded

Step 3: On plane B, draw an angle whose segments are the same length as the edges of the angle formed by planes A_1 and A_2.

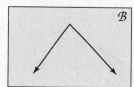

Step 4: Use your scissors to cut slits along the rays. Slip planes A_1 and A_2 through the slits. Label the angle in plane B as shown in the figure at the right.

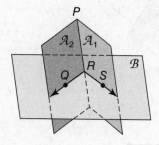

Answer each of the following.

1. What is the intersection of plane A_1 and plane A_2?

2. What is the intersection of plane A_1 and plane B?

3. What is the intersection of plane A_2 and plane B?

4. What do the answers to Exercises 1–3 have in common? What is the intersection of three planes?

5. Use planes C and D to construct a model in which the planes intersect as shown.

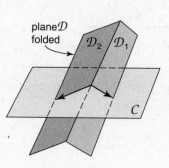

plane D folded

6. How does your construction differ from the first construction?

Geometry Lab Recording Sheet

(Use with Extend 1-1 on page 13 in the Student Edition)

Describing What You See

Materials:
straightedge

Exercises

Write a description for each figure.

1.

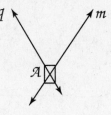

2.

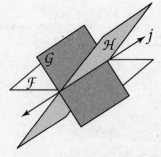

3.

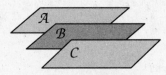

4. Draw and label a figure for the statement *Planes N and P contain line a.*

NAME _____ DATE _____ PERIOD _____

Using Overhead Manipulatives

(Use with Lesson 1-3)

Bisecting a Segment

Objective Bisect a line segment.

Materials
• straightedge
• transparency pens*
• compass*
• blank transparency

* = available in Overhead Manipulative Resources

Demonstration
Bisect a Segment

• Use the straightedge to draw a line segment. Label it $\overline{PQ}$.

• Open the compass to a setting that is longer than half the length of $\overline{PQ}$ Place the compass at P and draw a large arc.

• Using the same setting, place the compass at Q and draw a large arc to intersect the first.

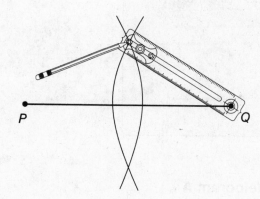

• Use the straightedge to draw a segment connecting the two intersection points. This segment intersects $\overline{PQ}$ Label the point of intersection M.

• Tell students that M bisects $\overline{PQ}$ Ask them how to verify this using a compass. **The same compass setting can be used for $\overline{PQ}$ and for $\overline{MQ}$.**

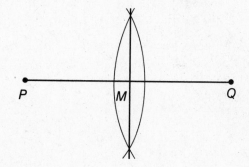

Geometry Lab

(Use with Lesson 1-3)

Pythagorean Puzzle

Square A

Square B

Square C

Triangle

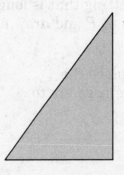

Parallelogram A

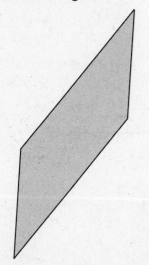

Parallelogram B

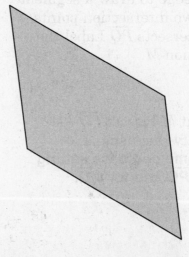

Cut out each figure on the previous page. Write the title for each shape on the back of the figure. Use the outline below to form each puzzle.

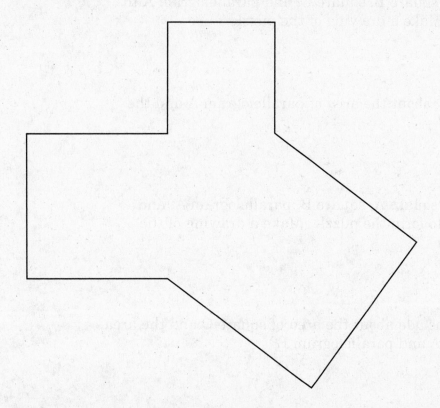

1. Use the triangle and square A, square B, and square C to form the puzzle. Make a drawing of the puzzle.

2. Compare the lengths of the sides of the squares with the lengths of the sides of the triangle.

3. Use the triangle, square A, square C, and parallelogram B to form the puzzle. Make a drawing of the puzzle.

Teaching Geometry with Manipulatives

4. What can you say about the area of parallelogram B and the area of square B?

5. Use the triangle, square B, square C, and parallelogram A to form the puzzle. Make a drawing of the puzzle.

6. What can you say about the area of parallelogram A and the area of square A?

7. Use the triangle, square A, square B, parallelogram A, and parallelogram B to form the puzzle. Make a drawing of the puzzle.

8. What can you conclude about the area of square C and the area of parallelogram A and parallelogram B?

9. Refer back to your conclusions in Exercises 4, 6, and 8 to complete each statement.

   area of square B = _____

   area of square A = _____

   area of parallelogram A + area of parallelogram B = _____

10. Substitute equal values of the last equation in Exercise 9 to write an equation that uses only the area of the squares.

11. Use the equation in Exercise 10 to make a conjecture about right triangles.

NAME _____ DATE _____ PERIOD _____

Using Overhead Manipulatives

(Use with Lesson 1-4)

Measuring Angles

Objective Measure angles by using a protractor.

Materials

- protractor*
- transparency pens*
- transparency prepared as described below

* = available in Overhead Manipulative Resources

Demonstration
Measure an Angle

- Prepare a transparency with the labeled angle as shown at the right. (Hint: Make the sides long enough to extend beyond the edge of the protractor. Answers will be given for an angle measuring 55°.)

- Show students the transparency. Ask students to name the angle. **∠K, ∠JKL, ∠LKJ, or, ∠1**

- Place the protractor over ∠JKL with the center point on vertex K. Discuss the markings on the protractor in relation to ∠JKL. Point out that the 0° line is not the same as the bottom of the protractor. Show students how you align the 0° mark on the protractor with side $\overrightarrow{KL}$.

- Locate the point on the protractor where $\overrightarrow{KJ}$ intersects the edge of the protractor. Ask students which edge to use when measuring this angle. **The scale that begins with 0 on the side where the 0° line is aligned with side $\overrightarrow{KL}$.** Have them read the measure of ∠JKL. **55°**

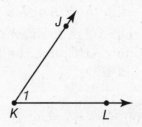

Extension
Draw an Angle

- Tell students they can also use a protractor to draw an angle with a specific measure. Have them draw ∠MNO if m∠MNO = 125°.

Using Overhead Manipulatives

(Use with Lesson 1-4)

Constructing Congruent Angles

> **Objective** Construct an angle congruent to a given angle.
>
> **Materials**
> - transparency pens*
> - compass*
> - straightedge
> - protractor*
> - blank transparency
>
> * = available in Overhead Manipulative Resources

Demonstration
Construct Congruent Angles

- Use the straightedge to draw an angle. Label it ∠ABC. Beside ∠ABC, use the straightedge to draw $\overline{XY}$.

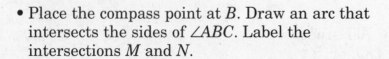

- Place the compass point at B. Draw an arc that intersects the sides of ∠ABC. Label the intersections M and N.

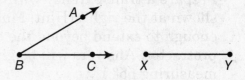

- Show students that you are keeping the same compass setting. Place the compass point at X and draw an arc that intersects $\overline{XY}$. Label this intersection P.

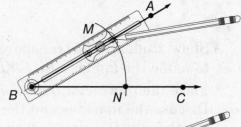

- On ∠ABC, set the compass at point N. Adjust the compass so that the tip of the pen is on M. Using the same compass setting, place the compass point at P, and draw an arc that intersects the larger arc you drew before. Label this intersection Q.

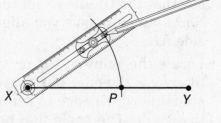

- Use the straightedge to draw $\overline{XQ}$.

- Use the protractor to measure ∠ABC and ∠QXP. Ask students if the angles are congruent. **yes** Ask students to describe the procedure you used to copy ∠ABC on $\overline{XY}$.

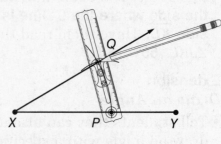

Sample answer: Find two points the same distance from B and copy the distance on $\overline{XY}$. Find the distance from M to N and copy the distance on the arc. Find the point where the arcs intersect and draw the ray.

Using Overhead Manipulatives

(Use with Lesson 1-4)

Constructing Angle Bisectors

Objective Construct the bisector of a given angle.

Materials

- transparency pens*
- compass*
- straightedge
- protractor*
- blank transparency

* = available in Overhead Manipulative Resources

Demonstration

Construct the Bisector of an Angle

- Use the straightedge to draw any angle. Label the vertex *B*. Place the compass at the vertex and draw a large arc that intersects both sides of the angle. Label these points *A* and *C*.

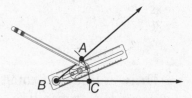

- Place the compass point at *A* and draw an arc to the right of *A*.

- Using the same compass setting and placing the compass point at *C*, draw an arc to intersect the one drawn from *A*. Label the intersection *D*. Ask students if the setting of the compass can be any length. **No; it must be longer than half the distance from *A* to *C*.**

- Draw $\overrightarrow{BD}$. Tell students that $\overrightarrow{BD}$ bisects ∠*ABC* Ask them how to verify this. **Measure ∠*ABD* and ∠*DBC* with a protractor.**

Extension

Double the Measure of an Angle

- Draw an acute angle and label the vertex *Y*. Draw a large arc through the sides of the angle and continue it to the left of *Y*. Label the intersection points *X* and *Z*.

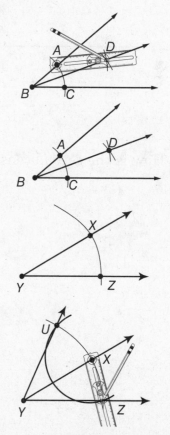

- Put the compass point at *X*. Adjust the setting so that it measures the distance from *X* to *Z*. Without removing the compass, draw an arc to intersect the large arc. Call this point *U*. Draw $\overrightarrow{YU}$. Ask students to describe the relationship between the measures of ∠*UYZ* and ∠*XYZ*. **The measure of ∠*UYZ* is twice the measure of ∠*XYZ*.**

Geometry Lab Recording Sheet

(Use with Extend 1-5 on page 55 in the Student Edition)

Constructing Perpendiculars

Materials
compass
straightedge

Model and Analyze the Results

1. Draw a line and construct a line perpendicular to it through a point on the line.

Draw a line and construct a line perpendicular to it through a point not on the line.

2. How is the second construction similar to the first one?

NAME _____ DATE _____ PERIOD _____

Geometry Lab Recording Sheet

(Use with Extend 1-7 on page 75 in the Student Edition)

Orthographic Drawings and Nets

Materials:
blocks
isometric dot paper
graph paper

Activity 1

Make a model of a figure given the orthographic drawing.

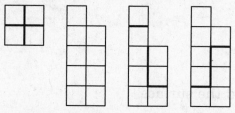

top view   left view   front view   right view

Activity 2

Make a model of a figure given the net.

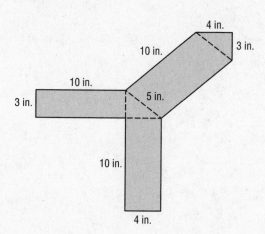

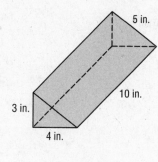

Model and Analyze

1. Make a model of a figure given the orthographic drawing. Then find the volume of the model.

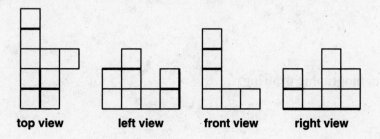

top view   left view   front view   right view

2. Make a model of a figure given the net. Then find the surface area of the model.

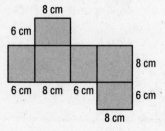

Reasoning and Proof
Teaching Notes and Overview

 Geometry Lab

If-Then Statements
(pp. 39–41 of this booklet)

Use With Lesson 2-3.

Objective Identify the if-then forms of conditional statements. State the converse of a conditional statement.

Materials
classroom set of Geometry Lab worksheets
scissors*
ruler*
*= available in Overhead Manipulative Resources

For this activity, divide the class into groups of three or four. Students first cut out the two triangles on the first page of the activity. Students then tear the angles from each triangle and form them in a straight line. This leads to the conclusion that the sum of the angles of a triangle is 180. While students complete the activity, encourage them to look for angle bisectors, how many right angles or obtuse angles are possible in one triangle, and the sum of the measures of two acute triangles.

As an extension, you may wish to have students use the conditional statements discussed in this activity to write formal two-column proofs.

Answers

1. 180;

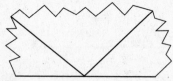

2. If a polygon is a triangle, then the sum of the measures of the angles is 180.

3. Sample answer: The sum of the 2 acute angles in a right triangle is 90°.

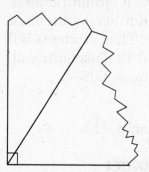

4. Sample answer: If a triangle is a right triangle, then the sum of the two acute angles is 90°.

5. Sample answer: If the sum of the two acute angles is 90°, then the triangle is a right triangle; true.

6. Sample answer: The supplement of the obtuse angle is the sum of the two acute angles.

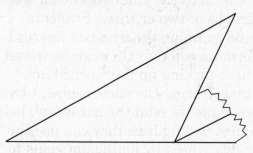

 **Geometry Lab
Recording Sheet**

Biconditional Statements
(p. 42 of this booklet)

Use With Extend 2-3. This corresponds to the activity on page 114 in the Student Edition.

Objective Learn to identify, use, and judge the validity of biconditional statements.

Materials

Students will write a biconditional statement as a conditional statement and as a converse. Then students will determine whether the biconditional statements are true or false.

Answers

See Teacher Edition p. 114.

Mini-Project

Tracing Strategy
(p. 43 of this booklet)

Use With Lesson 2-4.

Objective Determine whether a figure can be traced without picking up your pencil and without tracing the same segment twice.

For this activity, students should work in groups of two or three. Students should examine the first two figures to determine whether they can be traced without picking up their pencil and without tracing the same segment twice. Once students read the paragraph below the first two figures, they can use the rule discovered by mathematicians to determine whether Exercises 1–3 can be traced in such a manner.

Answers

1. yes; X

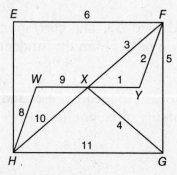

2. yes; A

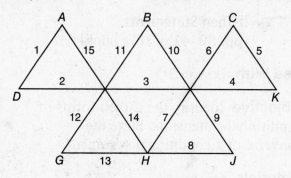

3. no

Geometry Lab Recording Sheet

Necessary and Sufficient Conditions
(p. 44 of this booklet)

Use With Explore 2-5. This corresponds to the activity on page 124 in the Student Edition.

Objective Determine necessary and sufficient conditions.

Materials

Students will analyze statements to determine whether they are true or false. Students will use the geometric ideas of necessary and sufficient conditions to determine the truthfulness of statements.

Answers

See Teacher Edition p. 124.

Geometry Lab

(Use with Lesson 2-3)

If-Then Statements

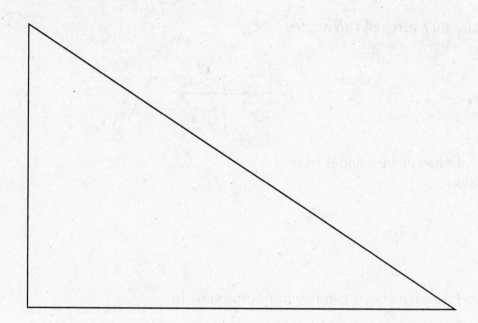

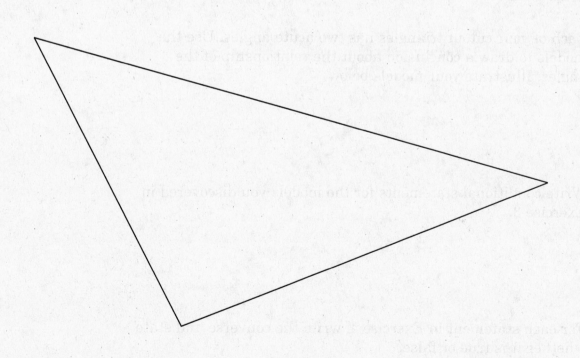

Cut out the triangles on the previous page. Tear the angles from each triangle as shown at the right.

1. What is the sum of the measures of the angles of the triangle?

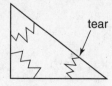

tear

At the right, draw a picture of the model that leads to your conclusion.

2. Write your answer to Exercise 1 as a conditional statement in the if-then form.

3. Each of your cutout triangles has two acute angles. Use the models to draw a conclusion about the relationship of the angles. Illustrate your models below.

4. Write conditional statements for the models you discovered in Exercise 3.

5. For each statement in Exercise 4, write the converse and state whether it is true or false.

6. Cut out one each of triangles A and B from the bottom of this page. Tear off the angles as you did for Exercises 1–5. As a group, make a hypothesis regarding each triangle. Then make a model of the hypothesis and draw a conclusion. Record the conditional statements in if-then form and explain why your statement is true. **NOTE:** You may compare the measure of each angle of the triangle with its supplement by extending a side of the triangle.

Triangle A   Triangle B

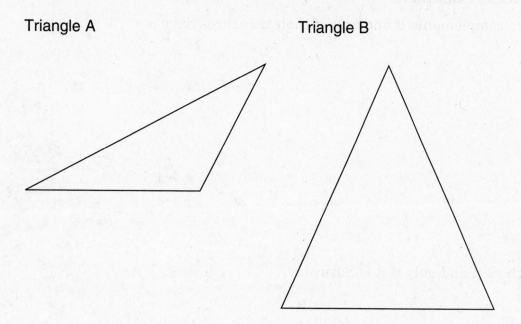

Triangle A   Triangle B

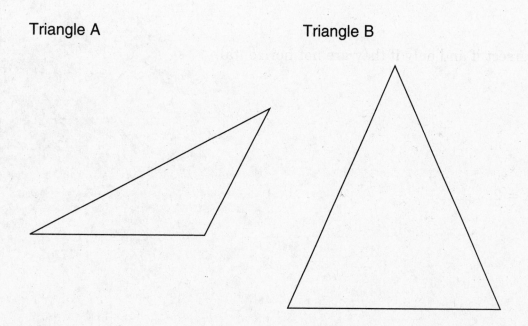

Geometry Lab Recording Sheet

(Use with Extend 2-3 on page 114 in the Student Edition)

Biconditional Statements

Materials: none

Exercises

Write each biconditional as a conditional and its converse. Then determine whether the biconditional is *true or false*. If false, give a counterexample.

1. Two angles are complements if and only if their measures have a sum of 90.

2. There is no school if and only if it is Saturday.

3. Two lines intersect if and only if they are not horizontal.

4. $|2x| = 4$ iff $x = 2$.

Mini-Project

(Use with Lesson 2-4)

Tracing Strategy

Try to trace over each of the figures below without picking up your pencil and without tracing the same segment twice.

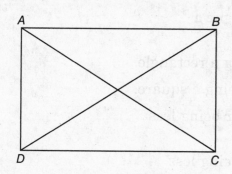

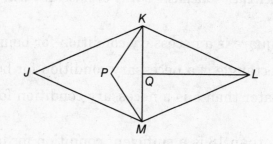

The figure at the left cannot be traced, but the one at the right can. Mathematicians have proved that a figure is traceable if it has no more than two points where an odd number of segments meet. The figure at the left has three segments meeting at each of the four corners. However, the figure at the right has only two points, *L* and *Q*, where an odd number of segments meet.

Determine whether each figure can be traced. If it can, then name the starting point and number the sides in the order they should be traced.

1.

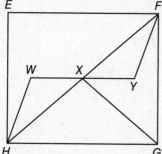

2.

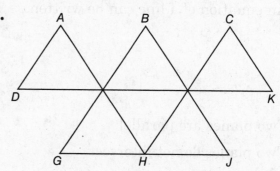

3.

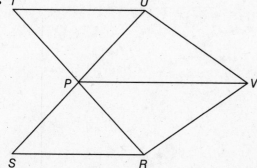

Geometry Lab Recording Sheet

(Use with Explore 2-5 on page 124 in the Student Edition)

Necessary and Sufficient Conditions

Materials: none

Exercises

Determine whether each statement is *true* or *false*. If false, give a counterexample.

1. Being a square is a necessary condition for being a rectangle.

2. Being a rectangle is a necessary condition for being a square.

3. Being greater than 5 is a necessary condition for being less than 10.

4. Being less than 18 is a sufficient condition for being less than 25.

5. Walking on four legs is a sufficient condition for being a dog.

6. Breathing air is a necessary condition for being a human being.

7. Being an equilateral rectangle is both a necessary and sufficient condition for being a square.

Determine whether I is a *necessary* condition for II, a *sufficient* condition for II, or *both*. Explain.

8.   **I.** Two points are given.

  II. An equation of a line can be written.

9.   **I.** Two planes are parallel.

  II. Two planes do not intersect.

10.   **I.** Two angles are acute.

  II. Two angles are complementary.

44

CHAPTER 3

Reasoning and Proof
Teaching Notes and Overview

Using Overhead Manipulatives

Parallels and Transversals
(p. 48 of this booklet)

Use With Lesson 3-1.

Objective Identify the relationships between pairs of angles formed by pairs of parallel lines and transversals.

Materials
lined paper transparency*
transparency pens*
protractor*
straightedge
* = available in Overhead Manipulative Resources

This demonstration involves discovering the relationships among the angles created by two parallel lines cut by a transversal. Once all angle pairs are identified, draw a set of vertical parallel lines cut by a transversal. Number the angles differently andquestion the students about all the angle pairs formed.

Answers
Answers appear on the teacher demonstration instructions on page 48.

 ## Geometry Lab

Graphing Lines in the Coordinate Plane
(pp. 49–50 of this booklet)

Use With Lesson 3-4.

Objective Graph parallel and perpendicular lines. Graph a line given its slope and *y*-intercept.

Materials
classroom set of Geometry Activity worksheets grid paper transparency
Pick-Up Sticks®
8–10 heavyweight pieces of paper, spinners, and brass fasteners
8–10 number cubes*
glue or tape
* = available in Overhead Manipulative Resources

For this activity, each group should attach one spinner grid from the worksheet to the heavyweight paper, using tape or glue. Have students complete the spinner according to the directions on the worksheet. Introduce the game Y ∪ X, and have the groups play the game. You may wish to have students play the game according to one of the variations on the worksheet.

Geometry Lab Recording Sheet

Equations of Perpendicular Bisectors
(p. 51 of this booklet)

Use With Extend 3-4. This corresponds to the activity on page 204 in the Student Edition.

Objective Explore figures on a coordinate plane.

Materials
grid paper

Students apply what they have learned about slope and equations of lines to find an equation for the perpendicular bisector of a line graphed on the coordinate plane.

Answers
See Teacher Edition p. 204.

Using Overhead Manipulatives

Constructing Parallel Lines
(p. 52 of this booklet)

Use With Lesson 3-5.

Objective Construct a line parallel to a given line through a point not on the line.

Materials
straightedge
transparency pens*
compass*
protractor*
blank transparency
* = available in Overhead Manipulative Resources

The demonstration involves constructing parallel lines. You may wish to have a student come to the overhead and use a protractor to verify that the lines are parallel.

In this extension, construct another line parallel to the ones constructed. You may wish to have students complete a construction of parallel lines at their desks.

Answers
Answers appear on the teacher demonstration instructions on page 52.

Using Overhead Manipulatives

Constructing Perpendicular Lines
(pp. 53–54 of this booklet)

Use With Lesson 3-6.

Objective Construct a line perpendicular to another line through a point on the line or through a point not on the line.

Materials
transparency pens*
compass*
straightedge
blank transparency
* = available in Overhead Manipulative Resources

There are two demonstrations for this activity.

• Demonstration 1 involves constructing a line perpendicular to another line through a point on the line. Ask why it is necessary to open the compass wider before you perform Step 3.

• Demonstration 2 involves constructing a line perpendicular to another line through a point not on the line.

• The extension is a discussion of how perpendiculars can be used to construct a square. You may wish to actually construct a square on a blank transparency.

Answers
Answers appear on the teacher demonstration instructions on pages 53–54.

Using Overhead Manipulatives

Parallels and Distance
(pp. 55–57 of this booklet)

Use With Lesson 3–6.

Objective Find the distance between two parallel lines.

Materials
TI–83/84 Plus graphing calculator
TI ViewScreen™, if available, or a blank transparency prepared as described
transparency pens*
compass*
straightedge
coordinate grids transparency*
* = available in Overhead Manipulative Resources

This activity includes two demonstrations for finding the distance between parallel lines. If you have a TI ViewScreen™, complete Demonstration 1. If you do not, complete Demonstration 2 using the coordinate grids transparency. You may choose to complete both demonstrations to illustrate each method to students.

• Demonstration 1 involves using a graphing calculator to find the distance between two lines. Discuss the reason for graphing the perpendicular line when you are trying to find the distance between the parallel lines.

• Demonstration 2 involves graphing the two parallel lines from Demonstration 1, $y = 3.5x + 8$ and $y = 3.5x - 7$, on the coordinate grids transparency. Then by construction, you graph the perpendicular line.

Answers
Answers appear on the teacher demonstration instructions on pages 55–57.

Using Overhead Manipulatives

(Use with Lesson 3-2)

Parallels and Transversals

Objective Identify the relationships between pairs of angles formed by pairs of parallel lines and transversals.

Materials
- lined paper transparency*
- transparency pens*
- protractor*
- straightedge

* = available in Overhead Manipulative Resources

Demonstration
Identify Relationship among Parallels and Transversals

- Show students the lined paper transparency. Tell them that the lines on the paper are all parallel to each other. Use the straightedge to draw two parallel lines using the lines on the transparency. Then draw a line, like the one shown below, that intersects the two parallel lines.

- Label the angles formed using the numbers 1 through 8. Have students measure each angle and record its measurement at the side of the transparency. $m\angle1 = 55$, $m\angle2 = 125$, $m\angle3 = 55$, $m\angle4 = 125$, $m\angle5 = 55$, $m\angle6 = 125$, $m\angle7 = 55$, $m\angle8 = 125$

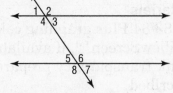

- On the drawing, use a different colored transparency pen to circle the numbers of all the angles that are congruent. **∠1, ∠3, ∠5, and ∠7 are congruent; ∠2, ∠4, ∠6, and ∠8 are congruent.**

- Tell students that ∠3, ∠4, ∠5, and ∠6 are examples of **interior angles**. Ask students which pairs of interior angles are congruent. **∠3 and ∠5 are congruent; ∠4 and ∠6 are congruent.** Tell them that congruent pairs of interior angles are called **alternate interior angles**.

- Ask students, "Which pairs of interior angles are supplementary?" **∠3 and ∠6 are supplementary; ∠4 and ∠5 are supplementary.** Tell them that interior supplementary angles are called **consecutive interior angles.**

- Tell students that ∠1, ∠2, ∠7, and ∠8 are examples of exterior angles. Ask students which pairs of exterior angles are congruent. **∠1 and ∠7 are congruent; ∠2 and ∠8 are congruent.** Tell them that congruent pairs of exterior angles are called **alternate exterior angles.**

- Ask students, "Which pairs of congruent angles are on the same side of the transversal?" **∠1, ∠5; ∠4, ∠8; ∠2, ∠6; ∠3, ∠7** Tell students that pairs of congruent angles that are on the same side of the transversal are called **corresponding angles.**

Geometry Lab

(Use with Lesson 3-4)

Graphing Lines in the Coordinate Plane

Y ∪ X Graph Game

A game of graphing lines on the Cartesian Coordinate System

Players: 2 to 4

Getting Ready to Play:

1. Before beginning the game, each group must construct a spinner. See the instructions on the next page.

2. Each player chooses 4 or 5 Pick-Up Sticks® to use for graphing lines. Each player should choose a different color, when possible.

3. Each player spins the Y ∪ X spinner. The player who spins a slope closer to zero plays first.

Rules:

1. Player 1 will spin the Y ∪ X spinner and determine the slope of the spin arrow. Next, the player will roll the die for a *y*-intercept.

Example:

 $m = 1$ $b = 2$

2. The player then graphs the line by placing a Pick-Up Stick® on the game board.

3. Players 2, 3, and 4 each take their turns.

4. The winner is determined by the first player to graph a line perpendicular or parallel to an axis or another line already graphed on the board.

Variations:

1. Players may wish to record the linear equations to verify the winning line algebraically.

2. Points may be awarded for parallel and perpendicular lines until all the sticks have been placed on the board. The player with the most points wins.

Spinner

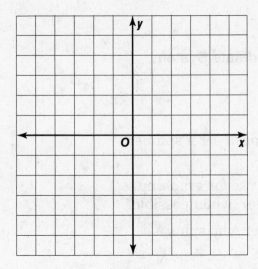

Assembly of Spinner

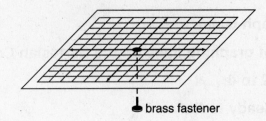

brass fastener

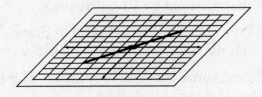

Game Board

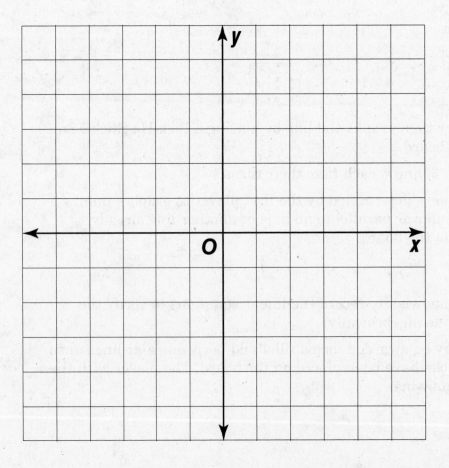

Teaching Geometry with Manipulatives

Geometry Lab Recording Sheet

(Use with Extend 3-4 on page 204 in the Student Edition)

Equations of Perpendicular Bisectors

Materials
grid paper

Exercises

Find the equation of the perpendicular bisector $\overline{PQ}$ for the given endpoints.

1. $P(5, 2)$, $Q(7, 4)$ **2.** $P(-3, 9)$, $Q(-1, 5)$ **3.** $P(-6, -1)$, $Q(8, 7)$

4. $P(-2, 1)$, $Q(0, -3)$ **5.** $P(0, 1.6)$, $Q(0.5, 2.1)$ **6.** $P(-7, 3)$, $Q(5, 3)$

7. Extend what you have learned to find the equations of the lines that contain the sides of $\triangle XYZ$ with vertices $X(-2, 0)$, $Y(1, 3)$, and $Z(3, -1)$.

Using Overhead Manipulatives

(Use with Lesson 3-5)

Constructing Parallel Lines

Objective Construct a line parallel to a given line through a point not on the line.

Materials
- straightedge
- transparency pens*
- compass*
- protractor*
- blank transparency

* = available in Overhead Manipulative Resources

Demonstration
Construct a Parallel Line through a Point not on the Line

- Near the center of a blank transparency, draw a horizontal line 5 inches long. Label the line *m*.

- Use a different colored transparency pen for the next five steps. Mark a point *N*, not on *m*. Draw a line through *N* that intersects *m* as shown. Label the intersection point *D*.

- Place the compass point at *D* and draw an arc. Label the points *E* and *F* as shown below.

- With the same setting, place the compass point at *N* and draw an arc. Label point *G* as shown.

- Show students how you use the compass to measure the distance from *E* to *F*.

- With the same setting, place the compass point at *G* and draw an arc to intersect the one already drawn. Label this point *H*. Ask students how the distance from *E* to *F* compares to the distance from *G* to *H*. **It is the same.**

- Draw a line through *N* and *H* and label it line *n*. Say, "By construction, *n* is parallel to *m*."

- Review the types of congruent angles formed by parallel lines and a transversal. **alternate interior, alternate exterior, and corresponding** Ask students what type of angles you used to create the parallel lines. **corresponding angles**

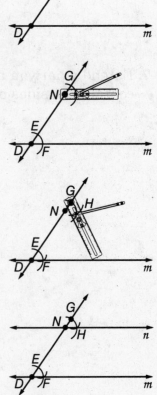

Extension
Construct Another Parallel Line

- Construct a line parallel to *m* below *n*. Label it *b*. Ask students what the relationship is between *n* and *b*. **They are parallel.**

Teaching Geometry with Manipulatives

Using Overhead Manipulatives

(Use with Lesson 3-6)

Constructing Perpendicular Lines

Objective Construct a line perpendicular to another line through a point on the line or through a point not on the line.

Materials

- transparency pens*
- compass*
- straightedge
- blank transparency

* = available in Overhead Manipulative Resources

Demonstration 1

Construct a Line Perpendicular to Another Line through a Point on the Line

- Draw a line and label it *a*. Choose a point on the line and label it *X*.

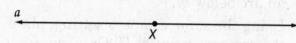

- Place the compass point on *X* and draw arcs to intersect line *a* on both sides of *X*. Label these points *R* and *S*.

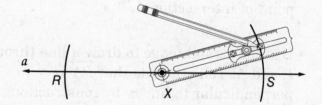

- Open the compass wider. Place the compass point at *R* and draw an arc above *X*. With the compass at the same setting, place the compass point at *S* and draw an arc that intersects the previous arc. Label this intersection point *Y*.

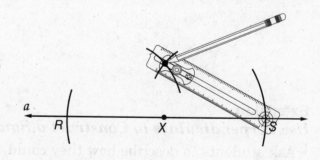

- Use the straightedge to draw a line through *X* and *Y*. Tell students that $\overleftrightarrow{XY}$ is perpendicular to line *a* by construction.

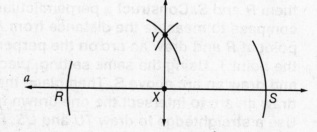

Demonstration 2

Construct a Line Perpendicular to Another Line through a Point not on the Line

- Draw a line and label it *m*. Choose any point above *m* and label it *P*.

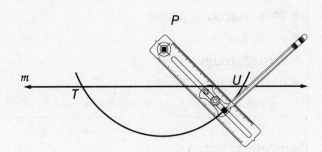

- Open the compass to a width greater than the shortest distance from *P* to *m*. Draw a large arc to intersect *m* twice. Label these points of intersection *T* and *U*.

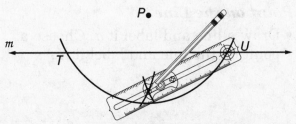

- Place the compass point at *T* and draw an arc below *m*.
- Using the same compass setting, place the compass point at *U*. Draw an arc to intersect the one drawn from *T*. Label this point of intersection *A*.

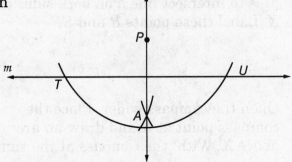

- Use the straightedge to draw a line through *P* and *A*. Tell students that $\overleftrightarrow{PA}$ is perpendicular to line *m* by construction.

Extension

Use Perpendiculars to Construct a Square

- Ask students to describe how they could use perpendiculars to construct a square. **Sample answer: Choose any two points on a line. Label them *R* and *S*. Construct a perpendicular through *R*. Use a compass to measure the distance from *R* to *S*. Place the compass point at *R* and draw an arc on the perpendicular through *R*. Label the point *T*. Using the same setting, place the compass point at *T* and draw an arc above S. Then place the compass point at *S* and draw an arc to intersect the one drawn from *T*. Call this point *U*. Use a straightedge to draw $\overline{TU}$ and $\overline{US}$. Figure *RSUT* is a square.**

54 *Teaching Geometry with Manipulatives*

Using Overhead Manipulatives

(Use with Lesson 3-6)

Parallels and Distance

Objective Find the distance between two parallel lines.

Materials

- TI-83/84 Plus graphing calculator
- TI ViewScreen™, if available, or a blank transparency prepared as described below
- transparency pens*
- compass*
- straightedge
- coordinate grids transparency*

* = available in Overhead Manipulative Resources

Demonstration 1
Find Distance Using a Graphing Calculator

- If a TI ViewScreen™ is not available, use Demonstration 2. If you have graphing calculators that are not TI-83/84 Plus, adjust the given keystrokes for your calculator.

- Set the axes ranges by entering the following keystrokes (TI–83/84 Plus).

  WINDOW (−) 4 5 ENTER 1 ENTER (−)
  3 ENTER 3 ENTER 1 ENTER 1 2nd [QUIT]

- Then graph $y = 3.5x + 8$, $y = 3.5x - 7$, and $y = -\frac{2}{7}x + \frac{4}{7}$ by entering the following keystrokes.

  Y= 3.5 X,T,θ + 8 ENTER 3.5 X,T,θ − 7 ENTER
  ((−) 2 ÷ 7) X,T,θ + (4 ÷ 7)

- Tell students that the first two equations will graph parallel lines because their slopes are the same. Ask students to explain how the slope of the third line relates to the slope of the first two. **It is the negative reciprocal because $3.5 = \frac{7}{2}$ and the negative reciprocal of $\frac{7}{2}$ is $-\frac{2}{7}$.** Ask students how this will affect the graph of the third line. **It will be perpendicular to the other two lines.**

- Remind students that when a line intersects a pair of parallel lines it is called a transversal.

55

Teaching Geometry with Manipulatives

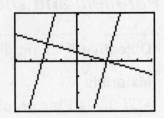

- Press GRAPH to display the three lines.

- Press TRACE , then ▲ on the TI–83/84 Plus. Move the cursor left to the point where the transversal intersects the parallel line. Ask students what the coordinates of this point are. **(22, 1)** Record the coordinates. Move the cursor right to the point where the transversal intersects the other parallel line. Ask students what the coordinates of this point are. **(2, 0)** Record the coordinates.

- Ask students to use the Distance Formula to find the distance between the two parallel lines. You may wish to refer students to the Distance Formula in Lesson 1-3 of *Glencoe Geometry*. **The distance between the parallel lines is $\sqrt{17}$ or about 4.1 units.**

Demonstration 2
Find Distance Using a Compass and Straightedge

- Copy the graphs shown on the coordinate grid transparency.

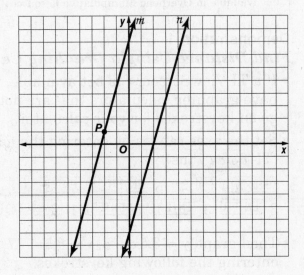

- Tell students that you are going to construct a line perpendicular to line *n* through point $P(-2, 1)$.

- Place the compass point at *P*. Make the setting wide enough so that when an arc is drawn, it intersects *n* in two places. Label these points of intersection *Q* and *R*.

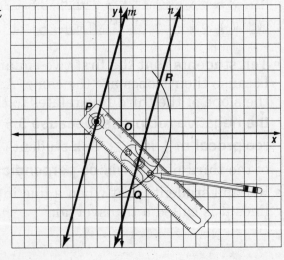

56

- Using the same compass setting, place the compass point at R and draw an arc below the x-axis and to the right of the previous arc. Then, still using the same compass setting, place the compass point at Q and draw an arc to intersect the one drawn from R. Label the point of intersection S.

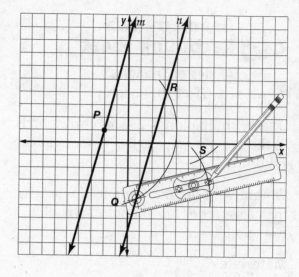

- Draw $\overleftrightarrow{PS}$. Tell students that $\overleftrightarrow{PS}$ is perpendicular to line m by construction.

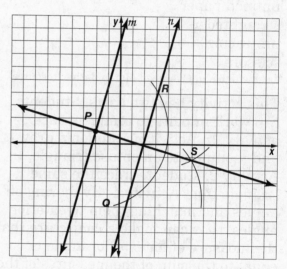

- Ask students, "Where does $\overleftrightarrow{PS}$ intersect line n?" **(2, 0)** Tell students to find the distance between lines m and n by using the Distance Formula. You may wish to refer students to the Distance Formula in Lesson 1-3 of *Glencoe Geometry*. **The distance between m and n is $\sqrt{17}$ or about 4.1 units.**

Congruent Triangles
Teaching Notes and Overview

Geometry Lab Recording Sheet

Angles of Triangles
(p. 61 of this booklet)

Use With Explore 4-2. This corresponds to the activity on page 243 in the Student Edition.

Objective Find the relationships among the measures of the interior angles of a triangle.

Materials
unlined paper
straightedge
protractor*
scissors
* = available in Overhead Manipulative Resources

This activity has two parts. Students can work in pairs to complete each activity. In Activity 1, students draw and manipulate an obtuse triangle. In Activity 2, students trace the same triangle from Activity 1. By tearing off angles and matching them to exterior angles, they can make a conjecture that the measure of an exterior angle is equal to the sum of the measures of the two remote interior angles.

Answers
See Teacher Edition page 243.

Using Overhead Manipulatives

Angle Measures in Triangles
(p. 62 of this booklet)

Use With Lesson 4-2.

Objective Discover the sum of the measures of the angles in a triangle.

Materials
transparency pens*
scissors*
tape
straightedge
paper
blank transparency
* = available in Overhead Manipulative Resources

This demonstration involves discovering that the sum of the angle measures of a triangle is 180.

Answers
Answers appear on the teacher demonstration instructions on page 69.

Using Overhead Manipulatives

Congruent Triangles
(p. 63 of this booklet)

Use With Lesson 4-3.

Objective Identify congruent triangles and corresponding parts of congruent triangles.

Materials
scissors*
transparency pens*
blank transparency
* = available in Overhead Manipulative Resources

This demonstration serves as an introduction for identifying and naming corresponding parts of congruent triangles. You may wish to create another example by drawing different triangles on the transparency and labeling them with different letters.

Answers
Answers appear on the teacher demonstration instructions on page 63.

Geometry Lab

Congruent Triangles
(pp. 64–65 of this booklet)

Use With Lesson 4-3.

Objective Identify the corresponding parts of congruent triangles.

Materials
classroom set of Geometry Lab worksheets
protractor*
tracing paper
scissors*
* = available in Overhead Manipulative Resources

Students begin this activity by measuring the angles of the three triangles on the worksheet. Then they prove that $\triangle ABC \cong \triangle XYZ$ and name their congruent parts. Students then trace and cut out the two smaller triangles. By arranging the triangles inside $\triangle QRS$, students discover different congruence statements and congruent parts. You may wish to have a few volunteers draw their illustrations from Exercises 3–5 on the chalkboard or overhead.

Answers

1. $m\angle A = 30, m\angle B = 60, m\angle C = 90,$
    $m\angle X = 30, m\angle Y = 60, m\angle Z = 90,$
    $AB = 4\frac{5}{16}'', BC = 2\frac{3}{16}'', AC = 3\frac{13}{16}'',$
    $XY = 4\frac{5}{16}'', YZ = 2\frac{3}{16}'', XZ = 3\frac{13}{16}''$

2. $\triangle ABC \cong \triangle XYZ; \angle A \cong \angle X, \angle B \cong \angle Y, \angle C \cong \angle Z, \overline{AB} \cong \overline{XY}, \overline{AC} \cong \overline{XZ}, \overline{BC} \cong \overline{YZ}$

3–5. Answers will vary. Drawings may be any of the following, or a variation of the following.

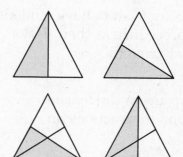

 Using Overhead Manipulatives

Tests for Congruent Triangles
(pp. 66–67 of this booklet)

Use With Lesson 4-4.

Objective Use SSS and SAS postulates to test for triangle congruence.

Materials
transparency pens*
compass*
straightedge
protractor*
5 blank transparencies
* = available in Overhead Manipulative Resources

This activity involves two demonstrations for creating congruent triangles.

• Demonstration 1 uses the SSS Postulate to prove that three constructed triangles are congruent. After you complete the first construction, you may wish to have students complete the next two constructions at their desks. You can then have a few students cut out their constructed triangles and lay them on the first triangle created on the overhead to verify that they are congruent.

• Demonstration 2 uses the SAS Postulate to prove that two constructed triangles are congruent.

Again, you may wish to have students repeat the procedure at their desks with the next triangle.

Answers
Answers appear on the teacher demonstration instructions on pages 66–67.

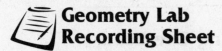

Geometry Lab Recording Sheet

Proving Constructions
(p. 68 of this booklet)

Use With Extend 4-4. This corresponds to the activity on page 271 in the Student Edition.

Objective Write proofs using constructions.

Materials
compass, straightedge, paper

Students will use constructions to write paragraph proofs and two-column proofs.

Answers
See Teacher Edition p. 271.

Geometry Lab Recording Sheet

Congruence in Right Triangles
(pp. 69–70 of this booklet)

Use With Extend 4-5. This corresponds to the activity on pages 281–282 in the Student Edition.

Objective Explore congruence in right triangles.

Materials
centimeter ruler*
compass*
protractor
* = available in Overhead Manipulative Resources

In Activity 1, students use a compass and centimeter ruler to construct a right triangle with given leg and hypotenuse measures. Students determine that this is a unique triangle. In Activity 2, students examine pairs of congruent right triangles and write congruence statements. Then students explore and prove theorems and statements regarding right triangle congruence. You may wish to select students to present their proofs for Exercises 10–14 on the chalkboard.

Answers
See Teacher Edition pages 281–282.

Mini-Project

Perimeters and Unknown Values
(p. 71 of this booklet)

Use With Lesson 4-6.

Objective Use algebra and the properties of isosceles triangles to find missing values and the perimeter of figures.

For this activity, students should work in pairs. In Exercises 1 and 2, students use algebra and the properties of isosceles triangles to find the missing values. In Exercise 3, students use algebra and the properties of isosceles triangles to find the value of x, and then to find the perimeter of the figure. In Exercise 4, students use algebra and congruent sides to find the perimeter of the figure.

Answers

1. 4; 9; 13

2. 26; 32

3. 73

4. 48

Geometry Lab Recording Sheet

(Use with the Explore 4-2 on page 209 in the Student Edition)

Angles of Triangles

Materials
unlined paper
straightedge
protractor
scissors

Analyze the Results

1. Angles *A*, *B*, and *C* are called *interior angles* of triangle *ABC*.

    What type of figure do these three angles form when joined together in Step 3.

2. **Make a conjecture** about the sum of the measures of the interior angles of a triangle.

Model and Analyze the Results

3. The angle adjacent to ∠*C*, is called an *exterior angle* of triangle *ABC*. **Make a conjecture** about the relationship of ∠*A*, ∠*B*, and the exterior angle at *C*.

4. Repeat the steps in Activity 2 for the exterior angles of ∠*A* and ∠*B* in each triangle.

5. **Make a conjecture** about the measure of an exterior angle and the sum of the measures of its nonadjacent interior angles.

61

Using Overhead Manipulatives

(Use with Lesson 4-2)

Angle Measures in Triangles

Objective Discover the sum of the measures of the angles in a triangle.

Materials
- transparency pens*
- scissors*
- tape
- straightedge
- paper
- blank transparency

* = available in Overhead Manipulative Resources

Demonstration
Find Angle Measures of a Triangle

- Prepare a large paper triangle similar to the one shown and cut it out. Trace the triangle on a blank transparency. Label the angles on both triangles X, Y, and Z. (Hint: The angles of the triangle should be large enough to measure easily.)

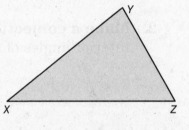

- Show students the paper triangle. Lay it on the transparency triangle to show that the triangles are congruent. Fasten the paper triangle to the transparency with a piece of tape in the middle of $\overline{XZ}$.

- Fold the paper triangle along a line parallel to $\overline{XZ}$ so vertex Y is on $\overline{XZ}$. Label this point Y' and label the endpoints of the segment formed by the fold A and B as shown.

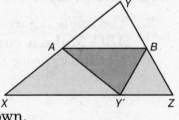

- Fold the paper triangle so that X and Z are on point Y' as shown.

- Ask students what is formed by $\angle XY'B$ and $\angle BY'Z$. **a linear pair** Tell students that since the angles of a linear pair are supplementary, $m\angle XY'B + m\angle BY'Z = 180$.

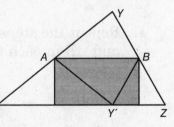

- Ask students what allows you to say that $m\angle XY'A + m\angle AY'B = m\angle XY'B$ **Angle Addition Postulate**

- Tell students to use substitution to find the sum of the angles of the triangle. $m\angle XY'A + m\angle AY'B + m\angle BY'Z = 180$

- Repeat this activity with a different triangle, or have students complete the activity at their desks. Then ask what they think is true about the measures of the angles of any triangle. **The sum of the measures of the angles of a triangle is 180.**

Using Overhead Manipulatives

(Use with Lesson 4-3)

Congruent Triangles

Objective Identify congruent triangles and corresponding parts of congruent triangles.

Materials

• scissors*

• transparency pens*

• blank transparency

* = available in Overhead Manipulative Resources

Demonstration

Identify Congruent Triangles

• If a colored transparency is available, trace, cut out, and label the triangles as shown. If you use a clear transparency, cut it in half. On each half, trace and label one of the triangles.

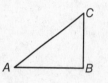

• Place the two triangles on the screen. Show students that the triangles can be matched exactly by placing one on top of the other and turning until all parts align. Tell students that this means that each part of the top triangle matches exactly the corresponding parts of the bottom triangle and that these triangles are congruent.

• Tell students, "The order of the letters in a congruence statement indicates the correspondence of the vertices." Ask students, "What angle corresponds to ∠*A*?" ∠***D*** Ask students, "what angle corresponds to ∠*B*?" ∠***E*** Ask students, "What angle corresponds to ∠*C*?" ∠***F***

• Ask students to state the congruence statement for the triangles. △***ABC*** ≅ △***DEF***

• Ask students to identify the three pairs of corresponding sides of the two triangles. $\overline{AB}$ **corresponds to** $\overline{DE}$, $\overline{BC}$ **corresponds to** $\overline{EF}$, **and** $\overline{AC}$ **corresponds to** $\overline{DF}$.

Geometry Lab
(Use with Lesson 4-3)

Congruent Triangles

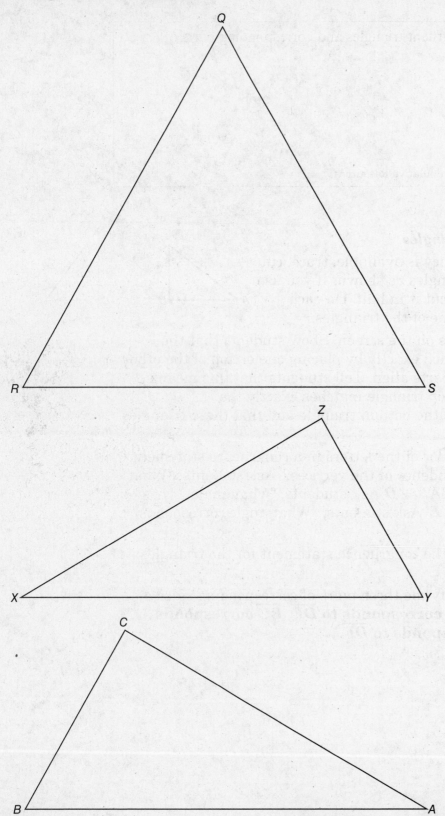

1. Use your protractor and ruler to measure each triangle.

$m\angle A =$ _____ $m\angle X =$ _____ $AB =$ _____
$XY =$ _____

$m\angle B =$ _____ $m\angle Y =$ _____ $BC =$ _____
$YZ =$ _____

$m\angle C =$ _____ $m\angle Z =$ _____ $AC =$ _____
$XZ =$ _____

2. Use the definition of congruent $\triangle$s to write a congruence statement. Name the congruent parts.

3. Trace $\triangle ABC$ and $\triangle XYZ$ on tracing paper. Label the vertices inside the triangles, and then cut out the triangles. Place the two triangles inside $\triangle QRS$ in any way. The triangles can overlap, but must be contained in $\triangle QRS$. Draw your figure and label the vertices. Name any congruent parts.

4. Reposition the two triangles inside $\triangle QRS$. Draw your figure and label the vertices.

What are the congruent angles and segments?

Were new triangles formed?

If so, name them. (Label new vertices where needed.)

Are there any congruent triangles?

If so, name them, making sure to use corresponding parts in your congruency statement.

5. Again, arrange the triangles to create a different pattern inside the equilateral triangle. Draw your figure and label the vertices.

What are the congruent angles and segments?

Were new triangles formed?

If so, name them.

Are there any congruent triangles?

If so, name them.

Using Overhead Manipulatives

(Use with Lesson 4-4)

Tests for Congruent Triangles

Objective Use SSS and SAS postulates to test for triangle congruence.

Materials
- transparency pens*
- compass*
- straightedge
- protractor*
- 5 blank transparencies

* = available in Overhead Manipulative Resources

Demonstration 1

Use SSS to Construct Congruent Triangles

- Tell students that you want to construct a triangle with sides of lengths 5 centimeters, 7 centimeters, and 8 centimeters.
- Draw a line and label it a. Then choose a point on a and label it X.
- Set the compass at 8 centimeters. Place the compass point on X and draw an arc to intersect a. Label the intersection point Y. Tell students that $XY = 8$ centimeters.

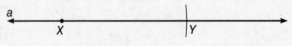

- Set the compass at 7 centimeters. Place the compass point on X and draw an arc above a.
- Set the compass point at 5 centimeters. Place the compass point on Y and draw an arc to intersect the one drawn from X. Label the intersection point of the two arcs Z.

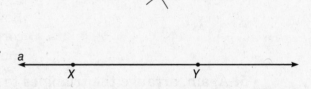

- Use the straightedge to draw $\overline{XZ}$ and $\overline{YZ}$.

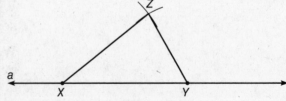

- Have students repeat the procedure with $XY = 7$ centimeters and then with $XY = 5$ centimeters. Ask them whether the triangles are congruent. **Yes, they were all made using the same compass settings.**
- Refer students to the SSS Postulate in Lesson 4-4 of *Glencoe Geometry*.

Demonstration 2
Use SAS to Construct Congruent Triangles

- Tell students that you want to construct a triangle with two sides of lengths 6 centimeters and 9 centimeters, and the angle formed by these two sides measures 60°.

- Draw a line and label it m. Then choose a point on m and label it R.

- Ask a student to use a protractor to draw a 60°-angle at R so that one side of the angle is on line m.

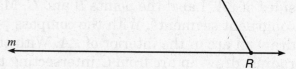

- Set the compass at 6 centimeters. Place the compass point at R and draw an arc to intersect the side of the 60°-angle that is not on line m. Label the point of intersection S.

- Set the compass at 9 centimeters. Place the compass point at R and draw an arc to intersect line m. Label this point of intersection T.

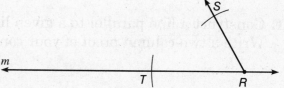

- Use a straightedge to draw $\overline{ST}$.

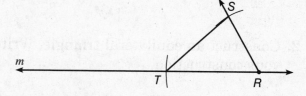

- Have students repeat the procedure with $RS = 9$ centimeters. Ask them whether the triangles are congruent. **yes**

- Refer students to the SAS Postulate in Lesson 4-4 of *Glencoe Geometry*.

Geometry Lab Recording Sheet

(Use with Extend 4-4 on page 271 in the Student Edition)

Proving Constructions

Materials: compass, straightedge, paper

Activity

Draw any angle with vertex *A*. Place the compass point at *A* and draw an arc that intersects both sides of ∠*A*. Label the points *B* and *C*. Mark the congruent segments. With the compass point at *B*, draw an arc in the interior of ∠*A*. With the same radius, draw an arc from *C* intersecting the first arc at *D*. Draw the segments $\overline{BD}$ and $\overline{CD}$. Mark the congruent segments. Draw $\overline{AD}$.

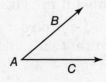

Exercises

Complete each construction using a straightedge and compass.

1. Construct a line parallel to a given line through a given point. Write a two-column proof of your construction.

2. Construct an equilateral triangle. Write a paragraph proof of your construction.

3. **CHALLENGE** Construct the bisector of a segment that is also perpendicular to the segment and write a two column proof of your construction. (*Hint*: You will need to use more than one pair of congruent triangles.)

Geometry Lab Recording Sheet

(Use with Extend 4-5 on pages 281–282 in the Student Edition)

Congruence in Right Triangles

Materials

centimeter ruler

compass

Analyze

1. Is each pair of triangles congruent? If so, which congruence theorem or postulate applies?

2. Rewrite the congruence rules from Exercise 1 using *leg*, (L), or *hypotenuse*, (H), to replace *side*. Omit the *A* for any right angle since we know that all right triangles contain a right angle and all right angles are congruent.

3. MAKE A CONJECTURE If you know that the corresponding legs of two right triangles are congruent, what other information do you need to declare the triangles congruent? Explain.

Activity

Construct right triangle *ABC* with a hypotenuse of 8 centimeters and a leg of 6 centimeters in the space provided.

Analyze

4. Does the model yield a unique triangle?

5. Can you use the lengths of the hypotenuse and a leg to show right triangles are congruent?

6. Make a conjecture about the case of SSA that exists for right triangles.

Exercises

Determine whether each pair of triangles is congruent. If yes, tell which postulate or theorem applies.

7. 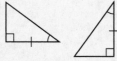 **8.** 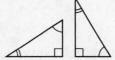 **9.**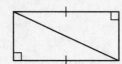

Proof. Write a paragraph proof for each of the following.

10. Theorem 4.6

11. Theorem 4.7

12. Theorem 4.8 (*Hint:* There are two possible cases.)

Use the figure at the right.

13. Given: $\overline{AB} \perp \overline{BC}, \overline{DC} \perp \overline{BC}$
        $\overline{AC} \cong \overline{BD}$
   Prove: $\overline{AB} \cong \overline{DC}$

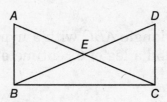

14. Given: $\overline{AB} \parallel \overline{DC}, \overline{AB} \perp \overline{BC}$
        E is the midpoint of $\overline{AC}$ and $\overline{BD}$.
   Prove: $\overline{AC} \cong \overline{DB}$

Mini-Project

(Use with Lesson 4-6)

Perimeters and Unknown Values

Work with a partner and discuss how to use the given information to find the unknown values in each of the following. Then find the values.

1.

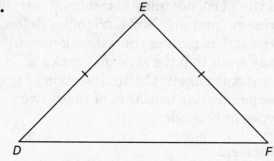

$DF = 3x + 1, DE = x + 5$
The perimeter is 31.
Find x, DE, and DF.

2.

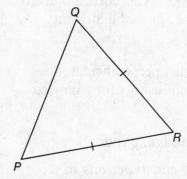

$PQ = x + 3, QR = x + 6$
The perimeter is 93.
Find x and PR.

3.

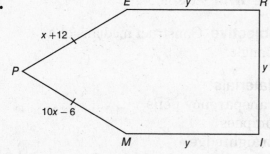

$y = 5x + 5$
Find the perimeter of the figure.

4.

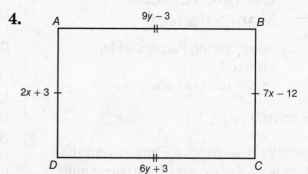

Find the perimeter of the figure.

Relationships in Triangles
Teaching Notes and Overview

 ### Geometry Lab Recording Sheet

Constructing Bisectors
(p. 76 of this booklet)

Use With Explore 5-1. This corresponds to the activity on page 321 in the Student Edition.

Objective Construct perpendicular bisectors and angle bisectors for triangles.

Materials
compass, straightedge, paper

Students will use constructions of perpendicular bisectors and angle bisectors to construct special segments in triangles.

Answers
See Teacher Edition p. 321.

Using Overhead Manipulatives

Investigating Perpendicular Bisectors
(p. 77 of this booklet)

Use With Lesson 5-1.

Objective Use paper folding to find the perpendicular bisectors of a triangle and investigate the relationships between the bisectors.

Materials
transparency pens*
protractor*
blank transparency
* = available in Overhead Manipulative Resources

This demonstration involves paper folding as a way to discover that the perpendicular bisectors of a triangle intersect at one point. While you are

completing the paper folding at the overhead, you may wish to have students complete the activity at their desk with a blank sheet of paper. In this extension, students use the same technique to find the intersection of the perpendicular bisectors of a right triangle and an obtuse triangle. Before students complete the extension, you may wish to have students make a conjecture about the intersection of the perpendicular bisectors of these two types of triangles.

Answers
Answers appear on the teacher demonstration instructions on page 77.

 ### Using Overhead Manipulatives

Constructing a Median in a Triangle
(p. 78 of this booklet)

Use With Lesson 5-2.

Objective Construct medians of a triangle.

Materials
transparency pens*
compass*
straightedge
blank transparency
* = available in Overhead Manipulative Resources

This demonstration involves using a compass and straightedge to construct a median of a triangle. Before the extension, you may wish to have two students come to the overhead and construct the other two medians of the triangle.
In this extension, students are to construct the medians of an acute triangle, obtuse triangle, and right triangle at their desks. To save on time,

you may wish to divide the class into thirds. Have each group construct the medians of one type of triangle. Then have students share their findings with the class.

Answers
Answers appear on the teacher demonstration instructions on page 78.

Geometry Lab
Special Segments in a Triangle
(pp. 79–80 of this booklet)

Use With Lesson 5-2.

Objective Identify and apply the definitions of angle bisectors, altitudes, and medians to congruent triangles.

Materials
classroom set of Geometry Lab worksheets
patty paper or waxed paper
construction paper

Have students begin by completing Exercises 1 and 2. While discussing the triangles drawn by students, you may wish to select students to draw the triangles they drew on the chalkboard or overhead.

Give each student two pieces of patty paper to use with Exercises 3 and 5. Have students complete the remaining exercises. For Exercise 6, you may wish to allow students to work in pairs. Tell students it may be helpful to use colored pencils to outline each different pair of congruent triangles.

Give each student a piece of construction paper. Have them cut out a triangle of any size. Instruct them to fold one side of the triangle so that the two vertices meet, and pinch a crease

on the midpoint. Fold a crease from the opposite vertex to the midpoint just found. Tell students that this segment is one median of the triangle. Have students repeat this process to find the other two medians of the triangle. Have students balance the triangle on a pencil point that is placed at the point of intersection of the medians. Ask students what this point of intersection is called. Explain that the centroid is the center of gravity of any triangle.

Answers
1a. Sample answer:

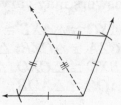

1b. Sample answer:

2a. Sample answer:

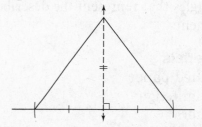

2b. Sample answer:

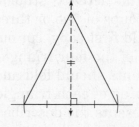

3.

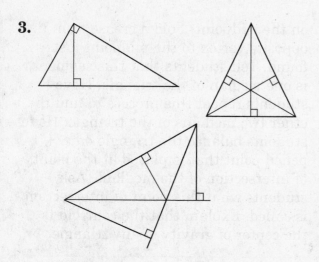

4. congruent (HL); nothing; nothing

5. Answers may vary.

6. $\triangle AXC \cong \triangle AXB \cong \triangle BYC \cong \triangle BYA \cong \triangle CZA \cong \triangle CZB$; $\triangle BQZ \cong \triangle CQY$; $\triangle BXQ \cong \triangle CXQ$; $\triangle AZQ \cong \triangle AYQ$; $\triangle AQC \cong \triangle AQB$

Mini-Project

Folding Triangles
(p. 81 of this booklet)

Use With Lesson 5-2.

Objective Copy, cut out, fold, and draw triangles that represent the described segments.

Materials
unlined paper
straightedge
scissors*

* = available in Overhead Manipulative Resources

For this activity, students should work in groups of two or three. Students should first copy, cut out, and label each of the four triangles. Then students should fold and make a drawing of each triangle that represents the described altitude, perpendicular bisector, angle bisector, or median.

Answers

1.
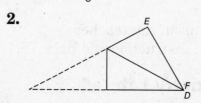

2.
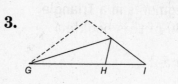

3.

4.
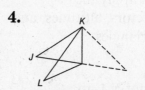

Geometry Lab Recording Sheet

Constructing Medians and Altitudes
(p. 82 of this booklet)

Use With Explore 5-2. This corresponds to the activity on page 332 in the Student Edition.

Objective Construct medians and altitudes for triangles.

Materials
compass, straightedge, paper

Students will use their knowledge of constructions to find the median of a triangle and the altitude of a triangle.

Answers
See Teacher Edition p. 332.

Using Overhead Manipulatives

Inequalities in Triangles
(p. 83 of this booklet)

Use With Lesson 5-5.

Objective Discover the relationships between sides and angles in a triangle.

Materials
lined paper transparency*
transparency pens*
protractor*
blank transparency
* = available in Overhead Manipulative Resources

This demonstration engages students in a hands-on method to discover the relationship among the sides and angles of a triangle. You may wish to choose one member from each of the three groups to write their side and angle measures on the chalkboard or overhead. This will aid in your discussion of the relationship between the sides and angles of a triangle.

Answers
Answers appear on the teacher demonstration instructions on page 83.

Using Overhead Manipulatives

Investigating the Triangle Inequality Theorem
(pp. 84–85 of this booklet)

Use With Lesson 5-5.

Objective Investigate the Triangle Inequality Theorem.

Materials
pipe cleaners or twist ties
centimeter ruler*

transparency pens*
lined paper transparency*
blank transparency
* = available in Overhead Manipulative Resources

This activity includes two demonstrations to investigate the Triangle Inequality Theorem.

• For Demonstration 1 make sure you have enough pipe cleaners or twist ties for students to complete the activity at their desks. This demonstration involves using a pipe cleaner or twist tie to discover lengths of sides that form triangles and lengths of sides that do not form triangles. Once students create their lists of triangles, they add the measures of the two shorter sides to discover that they must be greater than the third side in order to form a triangle.

• Demonstration 2 provides an example of how to find the range of the length of the third side of a triangle, given the lengths of two sides. After you complete the demonstration, you may wish to give students the lengths of two sides of a triangle and see if they can find the range for the length of the third side.

Answers
Answers appear on the teacher demonstration instructions on pages 84–85.

Geometry Lab Recording Sheet

(Use with Explore 5-1 on page 321 in the Student Edition)

Constructing Bisectors

Materials: compass, straightedge, paper

Model and Analyze

1. Construct the perpendicular bisectors of the other two sides of $\triangle MQP$. What do you notice about their intersections?

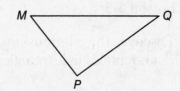

Repeat the two constructions for each type of triangle.

5. acute

6. obtuse

7. right

Using Overhead Manipulatives

(Use with Lesson 5-1)

Investigating Perpendicular Bisectors

Objective Use paper folding to find the perpendicular bisectors of a triangle and investigate the relationships between the bisectors.

Materials
- transparency pens*
- protractor*
- blank transparency

* = available in Overhead Manipulative Resources

Demonstration
Find Perpendicular Bisectors of a Triangle

- Draw an acute triangle *DEF* on a blank transparency. Fold the transparency so that one vertex falls on a second vertex as shown.

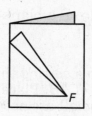

- Unfold the transparency and use a straightedge to draw a line on the fold.

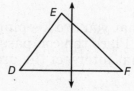

- Repeat the procedure with the other two pairs of vertices.
- Tell students that you have constructed the three perpendicular bisectors of the triangle. Ask students what they notice about the perpendicular bisectors. **They all intersect in one point.**

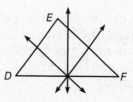

Extension
Find Perpendicular Bisectors of a Right Triangle and an Obtuse Triangle

- Have students draw a right triangle and an obtuse triangle on a piece of unlined or waxed paper. Then use the paper-folding technique to find the perpendicular bisectors. Is the result the same as for the acute triangle?
In the right triangle, the three lines intersect in a point on the hypotenuse. In the obtuse triangle, the lines intersect in a point outside of the triangle.

Using Overhead Manipulatives

(Use with Lesson 5-2)

Constructing a Median in a Triangle

Objective Construct medians of a triangle.

Materials
- transparency pens*
- compass*
- straightedge
- blank transparency

* = available in Overhead Manipulative Resources

Demonstration
Construct Medians of a Triangle

- Draw a large triangle on a blank transparency. Label the triangle ABC.

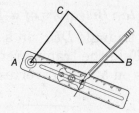

- Open the compass to a setting that is longer than half the length of $\overline{AB}$. Place the compass at point A. Draw a small arc above and below $\overline{AB}$.

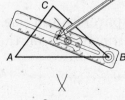

- Show students that you are keeping the same compass setting. Place the compass at point B and draw arcs that intersect the arcs you made from point A.

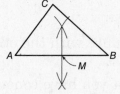

- Draw a segment connecting the points where the arcs intersect. This segment intersects $\overline{AB}$. Point out that this is the perpendicular bisector of $\overline{AB}$. Label the point of intersection point M.

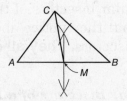

- Draw $\overline{MC}$. Tell students that $\overline{MC}$ is a median of $\triangle ABC$.

Extension
Construct Medians of an Acute Triangle

- Have students draw an acute triangle on a sheet of paper and construct all three medians. Ask them to describe any relationship they see as a result. **They all intersect at one point.** Have students construct the medians of a right triangle and of an obtuse triangle. Ask "Are the results the same?" **yes**

Geometry Lab

(Use with Lesson 5-2)

Special Segments in a Triangle

1. Using the dotted lines in each figure as angle bisectors, construct pairs of congruent triangles. Identify the rule for proving the triangles are congruent.

Example: **a.**   **b.**

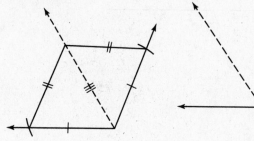

2. The dotted lines represent perpendicular bisectors of the segments. Draw segments to construct sets of congruent triangles. Then state the rule for proving the triangles congruent.

Example: **a.**   **b.**

3. Trace each triangle below onto waxed paper. Then make a crease along the altitude to each side. Sketch your waxed paper altitude lines on the triangles below.

4. Given: △*ABC* is isosceles with legs $\overline{AB}$ and $\overline{AC}$. What can be said about the two triangles formed by drawing an altitude from

vertex *A*? _____

vertex *B*? _____

vertex *C*? _____

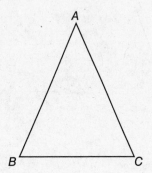

5. Construct a right triangle using the paper-folding techniques in this activity. Write instructions for your construction.

_____

_____

_____

6. In equilateral △*ABC* below, $\overline{AX}$, $\overline{BY}$, and $\overline{CZ}$ are altitudes. List all pairs of congruent triangles.

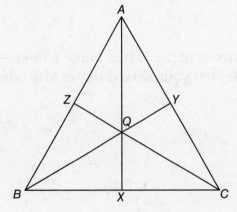

_____

_____

Teaching Geometry with Manipulatives

Mini-Project

(Use with Lesson 5-1)

Folding Triangles

Cut out a copy of each triangle. Label the vertices on the interior of the angle. Fold it so that the fold represents the segment described. Then make a drawing of the folded triangle.

Example: the altitude of $\triangle PQR$ from vertex P

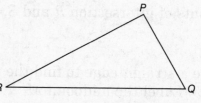

Fold the triangle <u>through</u> vertex P and perpendicular to $\overline{RQ}$. The folded side is the altitude of $\triangle PQR$ from P.

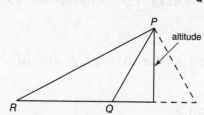

1. the altitude of isosceles $\triangle ABC$ through vertex angle C

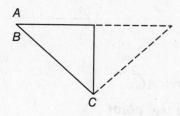

2. the perpendicular bisector of $\overline{DF}$

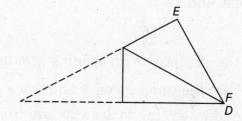

3. the bisector of angle G

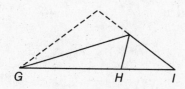

4. the median through vertex K

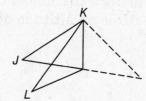

81

Geometry Lab Recording Sheet

(Use with Explore 5-2 on page 332 in the Student Edition)

Constructing Medians and Altitudes

Materials: compass, straightedge, paper

Construction 1

Step 1 Draw intersecting arcs above and below $\overline{DE}$. Label the points of intersection R and S.

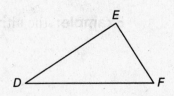

Step 2 Use a straightedge to find the point where $\overleftrightarrow{RS}$ intersects $\overline{DE}$. Label the midpoint M.

Step 3 Draw a line through F and M. $\overline{FM}$ is a median of $\triangle DEF$.

Construction 2

Step 1 Place the compass at vertex B and draw two arcs intersecting $\overline{AC}$. Label the points where the arcs intersect the side X and Y.

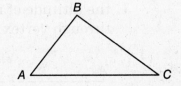

Step 2 Adjust the compass to an opening greater than $\frac{1}{2}XY$ Place the compass on X and draw an arc above $\overline{AC}$. Use the same setting to draw an arc from Y. Label the point of intersection of the arcs H.

Step 3 Use a straightedge to draw $\overleftrightarrow{BH}$. Label the point where $\overleftrightarrow{BH}$ intersects $\overline{AC}$ as D. $\overline{BD}$ is an altitude of $\triangle ABC$ and is perpendicular to $\overline{AC}$.

Model and Analyze

1. Construct the medians of the other two sides of $\triangle DEF$. What do you notice about the medians of a triangle?

2. Construct the altitudes to the other two sides of $\triangle ABC$. (*Hint:* You may need to extend the lines containing the sides of your triangle.) What do you observe?

Using Overhead Manipulatives

(Use with Lesson 5-5)

Inequalities in Triangles

Objective Discover the relationships between sides and angles in a triangle.

Materials
• lined paper transparency*
• transparency pens*
• protractor*
• blank transparency
* = available in Overhead Manipulative Resources

Demonstration
Discover Inequality Relationships in Triangles

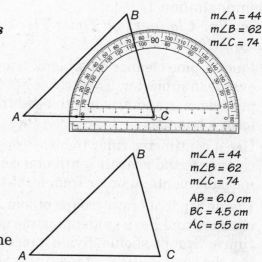

m∠A = 44
m∠B = 62
m∠C = 74

m∠A = 44
m∠B = 62
m∠C = 74
AB = 6.0 cm
BC = 4.5 cm
AC = 5.5 cm

• Draw a scalene triangle *ABC* on a blank transparency.

• Ask a student to measure each angle of the triangle with the protractor and write the angle measures on the transparency. (Sample measures are given.)

• Using the ruler edge of the protractor, have a student measure the length of each side of the triangle and write the lengths of the sides of the triangle on the transparency also. (Sample lengths are given.)

• List the angles and the sides in order from greatest to least.
  ∠C, ∠B, ∠A; $\overline{AB}, \overline{AC}, \overline{BC}$

• Divide the class into three groups. Have students in the first group draw an acute scalene triangle, students in the second group draw a right scalene triangle, and students in the third group draw an obtuse scalene triangle. Each student should label his or her triangle *ABC* and measure each angle and each side. Ask students to list the angles and sides in order from least to greatest.

• On the lined paper transparency, write the list of sides and angles from the triangle you drew on the first transparency. Ask volunteers to give the order of sides and angles found in their triangle until all of the orders are listed. Do students see a pattern? **The order of the angles corresponds to the order of the opposite sides.**

Using Overhead Manipulatives

(Use with Lesson 5-5)

Investigating the Triangle Inequality Theorem

> **Objective** Investigate the triangle inequality theorem.
>
> **Materials**
> • pipe cleaners or twist ties
> • centimeter ruler*
> • transparency pens*
> • lined paper transparency*
> • blank transparency
> * = available in Overhead Manipulative Resources

Demonstration 1
Use Pipe Cleaners or Twist Ties to Investigate the Triangle Inequality Theorem

• Place a pipe cleaner on a blank transparency on the overhead projector. Then choose two points on the pipe cleaner and attempt to bend the pipe cleaner to form a triangle.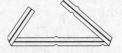

• Use a centimeter ruler to measure each segment of the pipe cleaner to the nearest tenth of a centimeter. Record the measurements in order from least to greatest on the transparency.

• Divide students into groups of four or five. Distribute pipe cleaners and have students perform the investigation several times. Groups should divide a piece of paper into two columns and list the combinations of measures that yield triangles on one side and the combinations that do not yield triangles on the other side. Each combination of measures should be written in order from least to greatest.

• After the groups have made a list of 15 combinations of measures, have students add the two lessor measures in each combination and compare the sum to the greatest measure. Ask students how the sum compares to the greatest measure in combinations that do not form a triangle. **The sum is less than or equal to the greatest measure.** Ask students how the sum compares to the greatest measure in combinations that do form a triangle. **The sum is greater than the greatest measure.**

Geometry—Chapter 5

Demonstration 2
Use Pipe Cleaners or Twist Ties to Investigate the Triangle Inequality Theorem

- Join two pipe cleaners at one end so that one measures 6 centimeters and the other measures 10 centimeters. Explain to students that these two segments represent two sides of a triangle.

- Move the two segments together slowly, explaining that the third side of the triangle is the segment between the endpoints of the segments. When the segments overlap, the figure becomes a segment. Measure the length from the end of the shorter pipe cleaner to the end of the longer pipe cleaner. **4 cm** Explain that the length of the third side of the triangle must be greater than 4 centimeters.

- Move the two segments apart again. When the two segments are stretched out to make a straight line, the figure becomes a segment again. Measure the segment from end to end. **16 cm** Explain that the length of the third side must be less than 16 centimeters.

- Tell students, "If the third side of the triangle is x centimeters long, we can write the inequality $4 < x + 16$." Ask students to check values of x in the ranges $x \le 4$, $4 < x < 16$, and $x \ge 16$ with the triangle inequality. Ask, "Does the solution check?" **yes**

Using Overhead Manipulatives

Investigating the Exterior Angles of a Convex Polygon
(p. 89 of this booklet)

Use With Lesson 6-1.

Objective Investigate the sum of the measures of the exterior angles of a convex polygon.

Materials
straightedge
protractor*
transparency pens*
regular polygons transparency*
blank transparency
* = available in Overhead Manipulative Resources

This demonstration involves finding the sum of the measures of the exterior angles of a convex polygon. Students begin by making a conjecture that the sum of the measures of the exterior angles is 360° for regular polygons. As students examine more polygons at their desks, they may alter their conjecture to include any convex polygon.

In this extension, students work with a partner to prove their conjecture. You may wish to ask a few students to share their proofs with the class.

Answers
Answers appear on the teacher demonstration instructions on page 89.

 ## Using Overhead Manipulatives

Tests for Parallelograms
(pp. 90–91 of this booklet)

Use With Lesson 6-3.

Objective Investigate conditions that ensure that a quadrilateral is a parallelogram.

Materials
pipe cleaners or twist ties
lined paper
geoboard*
geobands*
protractor*
blank transparency
* = available in Overhead Manipulative Resources

This activity includes two demonstrations that test whether a quadrilateral is a parallelogram.

• Demonstration 1 uses pipe cleaners or twist ties to construct a quadrilateral with opposite sides congruent. By measuring the angles of the quadrilateral, students discover that adjacent angles have a sum of 180, and therefore, opposite sides are parallel.

• Demonstration 2 uses a geoboard and geobands to form parallelograms. You may wish to have students come to the overhead and manipulate the geobands to form different parallelograms.

Answers
Answers appear on the teacher demonstration instructions on pages 90–91.

Using Overhead Manipulatives

Constructing a Rectangle
(p. 92 of this booklet)

Use With Lesson 6-4.

Objective Construct a rectangle.

Materials
compass*
straightedge
transparency pens*
blank transparency
* = available in Overhead Manipulative Resources

This demonstration involves using a compass and straightedge to construct a rectangle. You may wish to have students complete the construction at their desks while you complete the construction at the overhead. Discuss with students why the figure is both a rectangle and a parallelogram.

Answers

Answers appear on the teacher demonstration instructions on page 92.

Using Overhead Manipulatives

Constructing a Rhombus
(p. 93 of this booklet)

Use With Lesson 6-5.

Objective Construct a rhombus.

Materials
compass*
straightedge
transparency pens*
blank transparency
* = available in Overhead Manipulative Resources

This demonstration involves using a compass and straightedge to construct a rhombus. You may wish to have students complete the construction at their desks while you complete the construction at the overhead. Discuss with students how they can use the method for constructing a rectangle and constructing a rhombus to construct a square.

Answers

Answers appear on the teacher demonstration instructions on page 93.

Mini-Project

Square Search
(p. 94 of this booklet)

Use With Lesson 6-5.

Objective Determine the total number of squares in each figure.

Have students work in groups of two or three to count the number of squares in each figure. Tell students that it may be helpful to use colored pencils to trace each square as you count them. This may help prevent counting the same square more than once.

Answers

1. 55
2. 8
3. 22
4. 29

Geometry Lab

Linear Equations
(pp. 95–96 of this booklet)

Use With Lesson 6-5.

Objective Identify the quadrilateral formed by the midpoints of a quadrilateral as a parallelogram.

Materials
classroom set of Geometry Lab
worksheets
unlined paper
ruler*
scissors*
* = available in Overhead Manipulative Resources

In this activity, students use two different models to make a conjecture about the quadrilateral formed by the midpoints of a quadrilateral. For the first model, students cut out and fold the midpoints of each side of a quadrilateral. By measuring the lengths of the sides of the new quadrilateral formed by the folds, students discover that opposite sides are congruent. In the second model, students graph a quadrilateral on a coordinate grid. Then by using the Midpoint Formula and the Distance Formula, students discover again that opposite sides are congruent. Through both models and Theorem 8.9, students can make a conjecture that a parallelogram is formed by the midpoints of a quadrilateral.

Answers

1–5. See students' work.

6. Parallelogram; if both pairs of opposite sides of a quadrilateral are congruent, then the quadrilateral is a parallelogram.

7–12. See students' work.

13. Parallelogram; if both pairs of opposite sides of a quadrilateral are congruent, then the quadrilateral is a parallelogram.

14. A parallelogram is formed by the midpoints of a quadrilateral.

Using Overhead Manipulatives

(Use with Lesson 6-1)

Investigating the Exterior Angles of a Convex Polygon

> **Objective** Investigate the sum of the measures of the exterior angles of a convex polygon.
>
> **Materials**
> - straightedge
> - protractor*
> - transparency pens*
> - regular polygons transparency*
> - blank transparencies
>
> * = available in Overhead Manipulative Resources

Demonstration
Investigate the Exterior Angles of a Convex Polygon

- Place a blank transparency over the regular polygons transparency and trace the octagon.

- Using a different colored transparency pen, extend the sides of the octagon to form one exterior angle at each vertex.

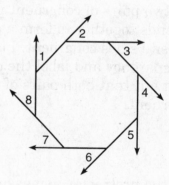

- Have students use a protractor to find the measure of each exterior angle. Then have them find the sum of the measures and record on the transparency.

- Repeat the process on a regular decagon and on a regular dodecagon.

- Ask students to make a conjecture about the sum of the measures of the exterior angles of a regular polygon. **The sum of the measures of the exterior angles is 360.**

- Have students work in pairs to draw a few more regular polygons to test their conjecture. Suggest that they try a nonregular polygon. Ask students if the result is the same. **yes**

Extension
Prove the Conjecture

- Have students work in pairs to prove their conjecture. Suggest that they consider the linear pairs of angles formed by the interior angles of the polygon and their corresponding exterior angles.

Using Overhead Manipulatives

(Use with Lesson 6-3)

Tests for Parallelograms

Objective Investigate some of the conditions that ensure that a quadrilateral is a parallelogram.

Materials

- pipe cleaners or twist ties
- lined paper
- geoboard*
- geobands*
- protractor*
- blank transparency

* = available in Overhead Manipulative Resources

Demonstration 1
Use Pipe Cleaners to Ensure a Quadrilateral is a Parallelogram

- Cut two pairs of congruent pipe cleaners and twist
  the ends together to form a quadrilateral with
  opposite sides congruent. Place on a blank
  transparency and label the quadrilateral *ABCD*.
  Point out that both pairs of opposite sides are
  congruent.

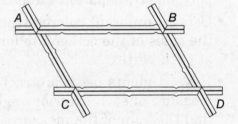

- Use the protractor to measure each angle
  in the quadrilateral. Record the angle
  measures on the transparency. (Sample
  measures are given.)

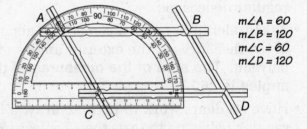

m∠A = 60
m∠B = 120
m∠C = 60
m∠D = 120

- Ask students what they notice about the measures of angles
  A and *C* and angles *B* and *D*. **They have a sum of 180.**
  What can they conclude about $\overline{AB}$ and $\overline{CD}$ and $\overline{AC}$ and $\overline{BD}$ as a
  result? $\overline{AB} \parallel \overline{CD}$ **and** $\overline{AB} \parallel \overline{BD}$ **since when cut by a transversal
  their consecutive interior angles are supplementary.** Therefore,
  the quadrilateral is a parallelogram by definition.
- Simultaneously pull on opposite vertices of the quadrilateral to
  change its shape. Then repeat the steps listed above. Is the result
  the same? **yes**

Demonstration 2
Use a Geoboard to Ensure a Quadrilateral is a Parallelogram

- Place the geoboard on the overhead. Place a geoband around pegs $L(2, 3)$ and $I(4, 4)$ using the numbers along the edges of the geoboard.

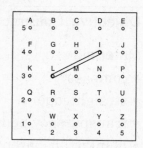

- Leaving the geoband around L and I, grasp the geoband and ask a student to tell you how many units to move up or down from L and I to form a parallelogram. Move the geoband accordingly.

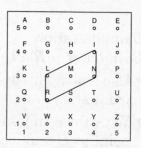

- Still holding the geoband, ask a second student to tell you how many units to move left or right from L and I. Move the geoband accordingly, and place the geoband around the points found. This will form a different parallelogram.

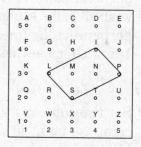

- The third and fourth points were found in such a way that segments between these points and L and I must be congruent and parallel. Why? **The number of units moved up or down and left or right determines the same slope and measure.** Ask students to verify that the slopes and measure of these segments are equal. Point out that this means that this quadrilateral meets the conditions of the theorem that says that a quadrilateral with two opposite sides parallel and congruent is a parallelogram.

- Ask two more students to find the slopes of $\overline{LI}$ and the segment between the third and fourth points. The slopes are equal, so these segments are parallel. Thus, the quadrilateral is a parallelogram.

- You may wish to repeat the investigation with four student-generated points.

Using Overhead Manipulatives

(Use with Lesson 6-4)

Constructing a Rectangle

Objective Construct a rectangle.

Materials
- compass*
- straightedge
- transparency pens*
- blank transparency

* = available in Overhead Manipulative Resources

Demonstration
Construct a Rectangle

- Use a straightedge to draw a line a. Choose a point D on a.

- With the compass at 8 centimeters, place the point at D and locate point E on a so that $DE = 8$ centimeters. Construct lines perpendicular to a through D and E. You may wish to refer students to the construction of a perpendicular line through a point in Lesson 1-5 of *Glencoe Geometry*. Label the lines b and c.

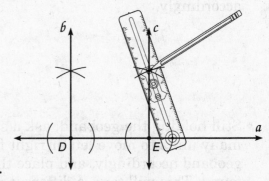

- Set the compass to 5 centimeters. Place the compass point at D and mark off a segment on b. Using the same compass setting, place the compass point at E and mark a segment on c. Label these points F and G, respectively.

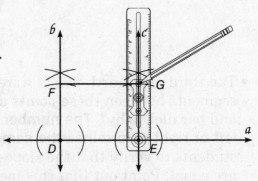

- Use a straightedge to draw $\overline{FG}$.

- Ask students to explain why *DEGF* is a parallelogram.
  $\overline{DF} \parallel \overline{EG}$ since each is perpendicular to a, and if two lines are perpendicular to the same line, then they are parallel. $\overline{DF} \cong \overline{EG}$ by construction. Therefore, *DEGF* is a parallelogram because two opposite sides are parallel and congruent.

- Ask the students to explain why *DEGF* is a rectangle.
  Quadrilateral *DEGF* is a parallelogram and all angles are right angles.

![overhead projector icon]

Using Overhead Manipulatives

(Use with Lesson 6-5)

Constructing a Rectangle

Objective Construct a rhombus.

Materials
- compass*
- straightedge
- transparency pens*
- blank transparency

* = available in Overhead Manipulative Resources

Demonstration
Construct a Rhombus

- Draw $\overline{WZ}$. Set the compass to match the length of $\overline{WZ}$. Use this compass setting for all arcs drawn.

- Place the compass at point W and draw an arc above $\overline{WZ}$. Choose any point on the arc and label it X.

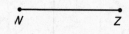

- Place the compass at point X and draw an arc to the right of X. Then place the compass at point Z and draw an arc to intersect the arc drawn from point X. Label the point of intersection Y.

- Use a straightedge to draw $\overline{WX}$, $\overline{XY}$, and $\overline{YZ}$.

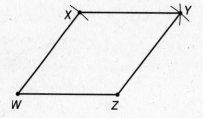

- Ask students to explain why $WXYZ$ is a rhombus.
  All four sides are congruent.

Mini-Project

(Use with Lesson 6-5)

Square Search

Work together to determine the total number of squares in each figure.

1.

2.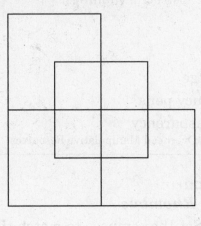

3.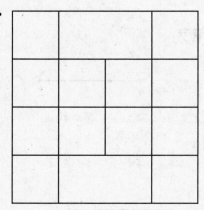

4.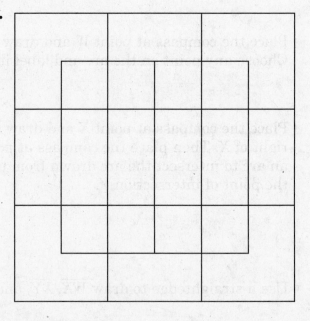

Teaching Geometry with Manipulatives

NAME _____ DATE _____ PERIOD _____

Geometry Lab

(Use with Lesson 6-7)

Linear Equations

1. On a separate piece of paper, draw quadrilateral *ABCD* with no two sides parallel or congruent. Cut out quadrilateral *ABCD*.

2. Fold to find the midpoint of $\overline{AB}$ and pinch to make a crease at the point. Mark the point with a pencil.

3. Fold to find the midpoints of, $\overline{BC}$, $\overline{CD}$ and $\overline{DA}$. Mark the points.

4. Draw the quadrilateral formed by the midpoints of the segments.

5. Measure each side of the quadrilateral determined by the midpoints. Record your measurements on the sides.

6. What type of quadrilateral do the folds in quadrilateral *ABCD* form? Justify your answer.

7. Graph a quadrilateral *WXYZ* with no two sides parallel or congruent on the coordinate grid.

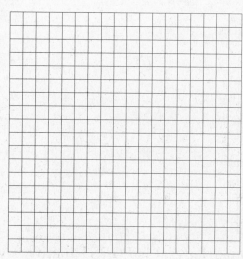

8. Use the Midpoint Formula to find the midpoint of $\overline{WX}$. Label the midpoint P.

9. Find the midpoints of $\overline{XY}$, $\overline{YZ}$, and $\overline{ZW}$. Label the midpoints Q, R, and S, respectively. Record the coordinates of the midpoints in the table.

Midpoint	Coordinates
P	
Q	
R	
S	

10. Draw $\overline{PQ}$, $\overline{QS}$, $\overline{RS}$, and $\overline{SP}$ to form a quadrilateral within $WXYZ$.

11. Use the Distance Formula to find the distance of $\overline{PQ}$.

12. Find the distance of $\overline{QR}$, $\overline{RS}$, and $\overline{SP}$. Record the distances in the table.

Side	Measure
$\overline{PQ}$	
$\overline{QR}$	
$\overline{RS}$	
$\overline{SP}$	

13. What type of quadrilateral is $PQRS$? Justify your answer.

14. Make a conjecture about the type of quadrilateral formed by the midpoints of a quadrilateral.

Proportions and Similarity
Teaching Notes and Overview

Using Overhead Manipulatives

Similar Triangles
(p. 99 of this booklet)

Use With Lesson 7-3.

Objective Investigate the relationships between the measures of similar triangles.

Materials
centimeter ruler*
protractor*
transparency pens*
blank transparency

* = available in Overhead Manipulative Resources

This demonstration involves construction, measurement, and ratios in discovering the Angle-Angle similarity postulate.

Answers
Answers appear on the teacher demonstration instructions on page 99.

Geometry Lab

Similar Triangles
(pp. 100–102 of this booklet)

Use With Lesson 7-3.

Objective Determine measurements of sides and angles of similar triangles using indirect measurement techniques.

Materials
classroom set of Geometry Lab worksheets
classroom set of mirrors, approximately 3-inch square
transparency master of Geometry Lab
blank transparency
You may wish to complete the following demonstration before handing out the worksheet.

Demonstration

Display the transparency master of 30°-60°-90° triangles on the overhead. On a blank transparency, draw more 30°-60°-90° triangles of different sizes. Overlap the triangles in various ways and discuss the characteristics of similar triangles. For each pair of similar triangles you illustrate, overlap the angles to show they are congruent.

Model Figures 1-3 one at a time on the overhead. Label the vertices of each triangle. Have students identify the corresponding angles of similar triangles.

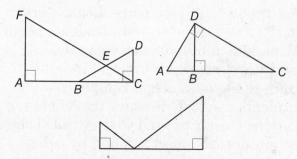

Hand out the worksheets and have students examine the diagram. Discuss the corresponding angles of the similar triangles. Explain which angle is the angle of incidence and which is the angle of reflection.

Answers

1–8. See students' work.

  9. far away from the mirror; closer to the object: angle became greater; farther from object: angle became smaller

 10. very tall: angle became very small, very short: angle became very great

 11. No; you must be able to adjust to see the top of the object.

Mini-Project
Measuring Height
(p. 103 of this booklet)

Use With Lesson 7-3.

Objective Make a hypsometer to measure the heights of various objects around your school.

Materials
heavy piece of cardboard at least 10 cm
  by 20 cm
straw
string about 25 cm long
small weight

For this activity, students should work in groups of three or four. Students begin by making a hypsometer using the cardboard, straw, string, and weight. Once the hypsometer is complete, students use it to measure the heights of various objects around your school. The height of each object is found by using similar triangles that are formed by the hypsometer and each object.

Answers
1–5. See students' work.

Using Overhead Manipulatives
Trisecting a Segment
(p. 104 of this booklet)

Use With Lesson 7-4.

Objective Trisect a segment.

Materials
compass*
straightedge
transparency pens*
blank transparency

* = available in Overhead Manipulative Resources

This demonstration involves using a compass and straightedge to trisect a segment. Once you complete the construction at the overhead, you may wish to have a student come to the overhead and use a ruler to verify that each of the three segments are congruent.

In this extension, students divide a segment into four congruent parts by construction. Have students use a ruler to verify that the segments are congruent.

Answers
Answers appear on the teacher demonstration instructions on page 104.

Geometry Lab Recording Sheet
Fractals
(pp. 105–106 of this booklet)

Use With Extend 7-5. This corresponds to the activity on pages 503–504 in the Student Edition.

Objective Draw a fractal tree.

Materials
isometric dot paper

Students will use iteration to study fractals. In Activity 1, students will draw an equilateral triangle. Then students will iterate the triangle using the midpoints of each side. In Activity 2, students will discover the numerical patterns in Pascal's triangle.

Answers
See Teacher Edition pp. 503–504.

NAME _____ DATE _____ PERIOD _____

Using Overhead Manipulatives

(Use with Lesson 7-3)

Similar Triangles

Objective Investigate the relationships between the measures of similar triangles.

Materials
- centimeter ruler*
- protractor*
- transparency pens*
- blank transparency

* = available in Overhead Manipulative Resources

Demonstration
Investigate Similar Triangles

- Use a protractor and a centimeter ruler to draw △RST with $m\angle T = 40$, RT 5 10 centimeters, and $m\angle R = 65$.

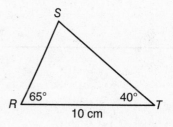

- Measure $\overline{SR}$. Then ask a student to find the value of $\frac{RT}{SR}$ with a calculator. **about 1.50**

- Draw △XYZ with $m\angle Z = 40$, $XZ = 6$ centimeters, and $m\angle X = 65$.

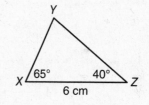

- Measure $\overline{YX}$ and ask a student to find $\frac{XZ}{YX}$. **about 1.5**

Ask students what they observe about these ratios. **They are the same for the two triangles.**

- Ask students to calculate $\frac{SS}{RT}$ and $\frac{YY}{XZ}$. Are they equal also? **about 0.71; yes**

- Ask, "Are $\frac{TS}{TR}$ and $\frac{ZY}{XZ}$ equal?" **about 1.07; yes**

- Ask, "How are $\overline{TR}$ and $\overline{ZX}$, and $\overline{SR}$ and $\overline{YX}$ related?" **They are corresponding sides of the triangles.**

- Divide students into groups of three or four. Have each group choose measures for $\angle A$ and $\angle B$ of △ABC. Each student in the group should choose a different measure for $\overline{AB}$ and draw a triangle. Then have each student find $\frac{AB}{AC}$, $\frac{BC}{AB}$, and $\frac{BC}{AC}$ and compare his or her ratios with those of other members of the group. **The ratios are all the same for the same pairs of sides.** Have students make a conjecture about two triangles that have two pairs of angles congruent.

Geometry Lab Transparency Master

(Use with Lesson 7-3)

Similar Triangles

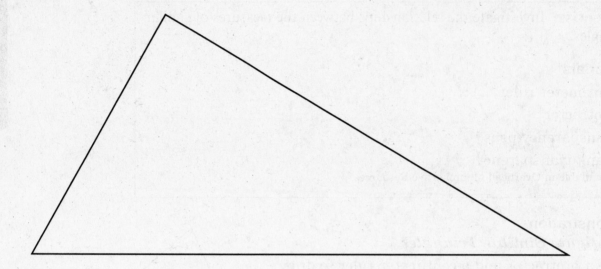

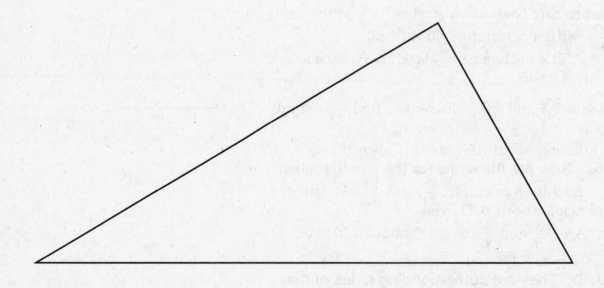

NAME _____ DATE _____ PERIOD _____

Geometry Lab
(Use with Lesson 7-3)

Similar Triangles

Measuring Instructions:

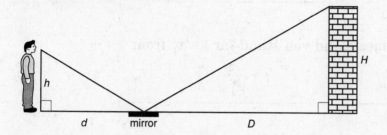

1. Place a mirror on a flat surface.

2. Stand erect. Do not lean over to view the mirror. While looking into the mirror, step forward or backward to view the top of the object.

3. Determine distance d and D. Use your pace, or step, length as an estimate. Then find your height (eye level).

4. Use the proportion $\dfrac{H}{D} = \dfrac{h}{d}$ to calculate H.

Use indirect measurement to find each of the following heights. (Draw a diagram for each problem.)

1. the school building

2. a tree

3. a goalpost

4. an electric pole

5. a sign

6. a flagpole

Choose your own objects for Exercises 7 and 8.

7. _____   8. _____

9. When measuring very tall objects, did you stand far away from or close to the mirror?

   _____

   How did the angle of incidence change as you moved the mirror closer to or farther from the object you measured?

   _____

10. What happened to your angle of incidence/reflection as your objects were very tall or very short?

    _____

11. Could all heights be measured using the same angle of incidence/reflection?

    _____

    Why or why not?

    _____

Mini-Project

(Use with Lesson 7-3)

Measuring Height

A hypsometer can be used to measure the height of an object. To construct your own hypsometer, you will need a heavy piece of cardboard at least 10 centimeters by 20 centimeters in dimension, a straw, a string about 25 centimeters long, and a small weight.

Mark off 1 centimeter increments on each of the 10-centimeter and 20-centimeter sides of the cardboard. Attach the straw to one of the 20-centimeter sides. Then attach the weight to one end of the string, and attach the other end of the string to one end of the straw, as shown in the figure below.

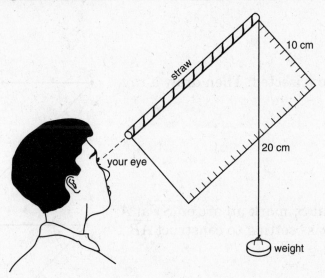

Sight through the straw to the top of the object. Note where the free-hanging string crosses the scale. Use similar triangles to find the height of the object.

Use your hypsometer to find the height of each of the following.

1. your school's flagpole

2. any tree on your school's property

3. the highest point on your school building

4. the goalposts on the football field

5. the hoop on the basketball court

Using Overhead Manipulatives

(Use with Lesson 7-4)

Trisecting a Segment

Objective Trisect a segment.

Materials
- compass*
- straightedge
- transparency pens*
- blank transparency

* = available in Overhead Manipulative Resources

Demonstration

Trisect a Segment

- Draw a segment *ST* to be trisected. Then draw a ray *SV*.

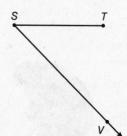

- With the compass point at *S*, mark an arc on $\overrightarrow{SV}$ at *A*. Then use the same compass setting to construct $\overline{AB}$ and $\overline{BC}$ so that $\overline{SA} \cong \overline{AB} \cong \overline{BC}$.

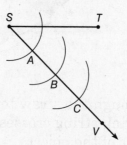

- Draw $\overline{CT}$. Then construct lines through *B* and *A* that are parallel to $\overline{CT}$. You may wish to refer students to the construction of a parallel line through a point not on the line in Lesson 3–5 of *Glencoe Geometry*. Call the points of intersection *Q* and *R*.

- Ask students why we can say that $\overline{SQ} \cong \overline{QR} \cong \overline{RT}$. **If parallel lines cut off congruent segments on one transversal, then they cut off congruent segments on every transversal.**

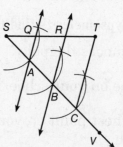

Extension

Divide a Segment into Four Congruent Parts

- Have students work in pairs to divide a segment into four congruent parts using the technique you demonstrated.

NAME _____ DATE _____ PERIOD _____

Geometry Lab Recording Sheet

(Use with Extend 7-5 on page 503-504 in the Student Edition)

Fractals

Materials:
isometric dot paper

Analyze the Results

1. If you continue the process, how many unshaded triangles will you have at Stage 3?

2. What is the perimeter of a unshaded triangle in Stage 4?

3. If you continue the process indefinitely, what will happen to the perimeters of the unshaded triangles?

4. **CHALLENGE** Complete the proof below.

   Given: $\triangle KAP$ is equilateral. *D, F, M, B, C,* and *E* are midpoints of $\overline{KA}$, $\overline{AP}$, $\overline{PK}$, $\overline{DA}$, $\overline{AF}$, and $\overline{FD}$, respectively.

   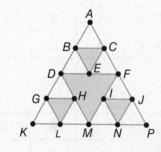

   Prove: $\triangle BAC \sim \triangle KAP$

5. A *fractal tree* can be drawn by making two new branches from the endpoint of each original branch, each one-third as long as the previous branch.

   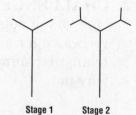

   Stage 1   Stage 2

a. Draw Stages 3 and 4 of a fractal tree. How many total branches do you have in Stages 1 through 4? (Do not count the stems.)

b. Write an expression to predict the number of branches at each stage.

Analyze the Results

6. Write a formula for the sum S of any row n in the Pascal Triangle.

7. What is the sum of the values in the eighth row of Pascal's Triangle?

Exercises
Write a recursive formula for $F(x)$.

8.

X	2	4	6	8	10
F(X)	3	7	11	15	19

9.

X	0	5	10	15	20
F(X)	0	20	90	210	380

10.

X	1	2	4	8	10
F(X)	1	0.5	0.25	0.125	1.0

11.

X	4	9	16	25	36
F(X)	5	6	7	8	9

12. CHALLENGE The pattern below represents a sequence of *triangular numbers*. How many dots will be in the 8th term in the sequence? Is it possible to write a recursive formula that can be used to determine the number of dots in the nth triangular number in the series? If so, write the formula. If not, explain why not.

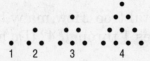

CHAPTER 8 Right Triangles and Trigonometry Teaching Notes and Overview

 ## Mini-Project

The Pythagorean Theorem
(p. 110 of this booklet)

Use With Lesson 8-2.

Objective Trace, cut out, and rearrange the six parts of the square to create an area model of the Pythagorean theorem.

Materials
unlined paper
straightedge
scissors*
* = available in Overhead Manipulative Resources

For this activity, students should work in pairs. Students begin by tracing and cutting out the six parts of the large square. Remind students to number each part. The students then rearrange the parts to form two smaller squares. By determining the area of the large square and the two smaller squares, the students discover another method to proving the Pythagorean theorem.

Answers

1. c^2

2.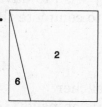

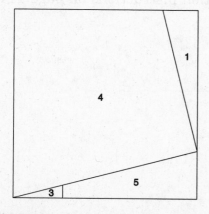

3. a^2; b^2

4. sum of areas of two smaller squares = area of larger square

5. yes

 ## Geometry Lab Recording Sheet

The Pythagorean Theorem
(p. 111 of this booklet)

Use With Explore 8-2. This corresponds to the activity on page 540 in the Student Edition.

Objective Physically explore side-length relationships in the Pythagorean Theorem.

Materials
patty paper or square pieces of tracing paper
ruler*
* = available in Overhead Manipulative Resources

For this activity, students can work in groups of two or three. Students draw and label the area of different regions on two pieces of patty paper. By shading equal areas on the two pieces of patty paper, students discover that $a^2 + b^2 = c^2$. Students then use a ruler to measure a, b, and c, and verify that $a^2 + b^2 = c^2$.

Answers
See Teacher Edition page 540.

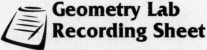 **Geometry Lab Recording Sheet**

Coordinates in Space
(pp. 112–113 of this booklet)

Use With Extend 8-2. This corresponds to the activity on pages 550–551 in the Student Edition.

Objective Graph points in space and use the distance and midpoint formulas in space.

Materials
none

Students will use the distance formula and the midpoint formula in space.

Answers
See Teacher Edition pp. 550–551.

 Using Overhead Manipulatives

The Pythagorean Theorem
(p. 114 of this booklet)

Use With Lesson 8-2.

Objective Find the relationship among the sides of a right triangle.

Materials
centimeter grids transparency*
straightedge
transparency pens*
scissors*
2 blank transparencies
* = available in Overhead Manipulative Resources

This demonstration is an area model of the Pythagorean Theorem. Show students how centimeter grid paper can be used as a ruler to find the measure of the hypotenuse. Ask students for other methods that could have been used to find the length of the hypotenuse.

In this extension, students explore the same technique with right, acute, and obtuse triangles. You may wish to have students work in groups to complete the extension.

Answers
Answers appear on the teacher demonstration instructions on page 114.

Geometry Lab
Trigonometry
(pp. 115–117 of this booklet)

Use With Lesson 8-4.

Objective Use indirect measurement as an application of trigonometric functions.

Materials
classroom set of Geometry Lab worksheets transparency master of Geometry Lab transparent tape
kite string
protractor*, 5″ × 7″ index card, straw, paper clip, and scientific calculator for each pair of students
* = available in Overhead Manipulative Resources

Prior to activity, assemble a model of a hypsometer according to the instructions on the transparency master.

Display the transparency master on the overhead and have pairs of students assemble a hypsometer of their own. Show students the hypsometer you made prior to class. If protractors are not available, you can use copies of the protractor model at the bottom of the transparency master.

Have students practice finding a horizontal line of sight and reading the hypsometer angle of inclination. Once students are comfortable using the hypsometer, have them complete the activity. You may wish to have students compare measurements and answers after they complete the activity.

Answers

1. ≈ 15.5 ft

2. ≈ 19.3 m

3–10. See students' work.

 Geometry Lab
Recording Sheet
Adding Vectors
(p. 118 of this booklet)

Use With Extend 8-7. This corresponds to the activity on page 601 in the Student Edition.

Objective Use scale drawings and direct measurement to find the resultant of two vectors.

Materials
ruler

Students will make a scale drawing of two vectors and find the resultant. Then students will find the magnitude and direction of the resultant.

Answers
See Teacher Edition p. 601.

109

Mini-Project

(Use with Lesson 8-2)

The Pythagorean Theorem

Trace the figure shown below and cut out the six parts. Then answer each of the following.

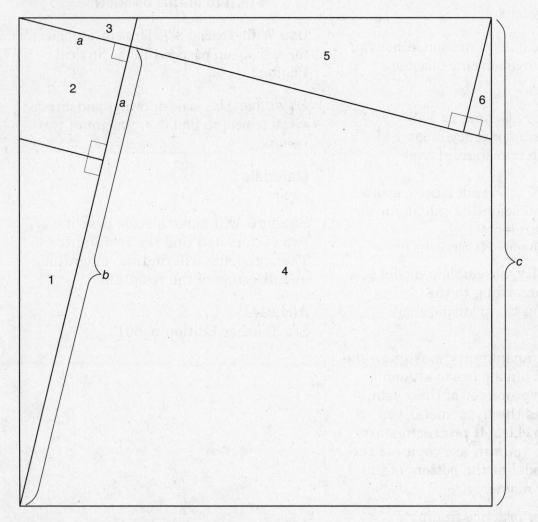

1. What is the area of the large square?

2. Show how two smaller squares can be made using all of the six parts.

3. What is the area of each of the smaller squares.

4. What is the relationship between the three squares.

5. Does $a^2 + b^2 = c^2$?

Geometry Lab Recording Sheet

(Use with Explore 8-2 on page 540 in the Student Edition)

The Pythagorean Theorem

Materials

patty paper or square pieces of tracing paper
ruler

Analyze the Results

1. Use a ruler to measure a, b, and c. Do these measures confirm that $a^2 + b^2 = c^2$?

2. Repeat the activity with different a and b values. What do you notice?

3. **WRITING IN MATH** Explain why the drawing at the right is an illustration of the Pythagorean Theorem.

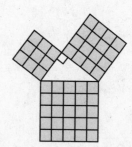

4. **CHALLENGE** Draw a geometric diagram to show that for any positive numbers a and b, $a + b > \sqrt{a^2 + b^2}$. Explain.

Geometry Lab Recording Sheet

(Use with Extend 8-2 on pages 550-551 in the Student Edition)

Coordinates in Space

Materials: none

Exercises

Graph a rectangular solid that contains the given point and the origin as vertices. Label the coordinates of each vertex.

1. $A(2, 1, 5)$

2. $P(-1, 4, 2)$

3. $C(-2, 2, 2)$

4. $R(3, -4, 1)$

5. $P(4, 6, -3)$

6. $G(4, 1, -3)$

7. $K(-2, -4, -4)$

8. $W(-1, -3, -6)$

9. $W(3, 3, 4)$

Exercises

Determine the distance between each pair of points. Then determine the coordinates of the midpoint M of the segment joining the pair of points.

10. $D(0, 0, 0)$ and $E(1, 5, 7)$

11. $G(-3, -4, 6)$ and $H(5, -3, -5)$

12. $K(2, 2, 0)$ and $L(-2, -2, 0)$

13. $P(-2, -5, 8)$ and $Q(3, -2, -1)$

14. $A(4, 7, 9)$ and $B(-3, 8, -8)$

15. $W(-12, 8, 10)$ and $Z(-4, 1, -2)$

16. $F\left(\dfrac{3}{5}, 0, \dfrac{4}{5}\right)$ and $G(0, 3, 0)$

17. $G(1, -1, 6)$ and $H\left(\dfrac{1}{5}, -\dfrac{2}{5}, 2\right)$

18. $B\left(\sqrt{3}, 2, 2\sqrt{2}\right)$ and $C\left(-2\sqrt{3}, 4, 4\sqrt{2}\right)$

19. $S\left(6\sqrt{3}, 4, 4\sqrt{2}\right)$ and $T\left(4\sqrt{3}, 5, \sqrt{2}\right)$

20. PROOF Write a coordinate proof of the Distance Formula in Space.
   Given: A has coordinates $A(x_1, y_1, z_1)$, and B has coordinates $B(x_2, y_2, z_2)$.
   Prove: $AB = \sqrt{(x_2 - x_1)^2 + (y_2 - y_1)^2 + (z_2 - z_1)^2}$

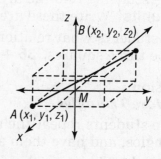

21. WRITING IN MATH Compare and contrast the Distance and Midpoint Formulas on the coordinate plane and in three-dimensional coordinate space.

113

Using Overhead Manipulatives

(Use with Lesson 8-2)

The Pythagorean Theorem

Objective Find the relationship among the sides of a right triangle.

Materials
- centimeter grids transparency*
- straightedge
- transparency pens*
- scissors*
- 2 blank transparencies

* = available in Overhead Manipulative Resources

Demonstration

Find a Triangle Relationship

- Place a blank transparency on the centimeter grid transparency. Use the straightedge to draw a segment 8 centimeters long. At one end of this segment, draw a perpendicular segment 6 centimeters long. Draw a third segment to form a triangle.

- Measure the length of the longest side of the triangle using the centimeter grid transparency. Ask students to state the length of this segment. **10 cm**

- On a blank transparency, draw three squares: one with 6 centimeters on a side, one with 8 centimeters on a side, and one with 10 centimeters on a side. Cut out the squares.

- Place the edges of each square against the corresponding side of the triangle.

- Ask students what kind of triangle was formed. **right triangle**

- Have students find the area of each square. **36 units², 64 units², 100 units²** Write these areas on the squares.

- Ask students what relationship exists among the areas of the three squares. **36 + 64 = 100**

Extension

Test More Triangles

- Have students repeat the activity for each of the following triangles, and have them summarize their findings.
  - right triangle with perpendicular sides 9 units and 12 units long
  - nonright acute triangle with sides 9 units and 12 units long
  - obtuse triangle with sides 9 units and 12 units long

The area of the square along the hypotenuse of the triangle is equal to the sum of the areas of the squares on the other two sides. The area of the square on the longest side of the acute triangle is less than the sum of the areas of the other two squares. The area of the square on the longest side of the obtuse triangle is greater than the sum of the areas of the other two squares.

Geometry Lab Transparency Master

(Use with Lesson 8-4)

Trigonometry

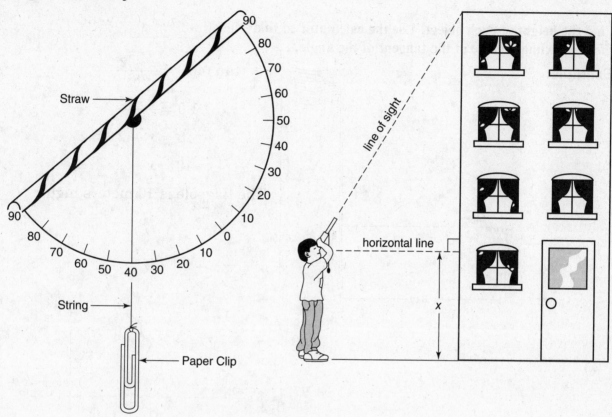

Place on the edge of the index card.

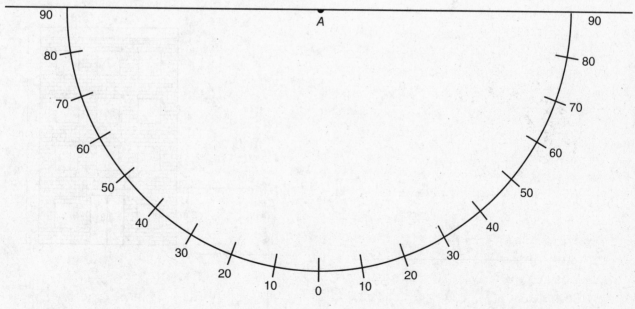

Geometry Lab

(Use with Lesson 8-4)

Trigonometry

Find the height of each object. Use the calculator to find
the approximate value of the tangent of the angle.

Example:

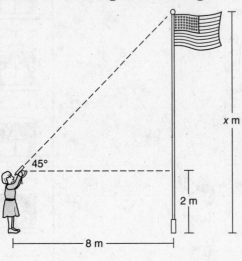

$$\tan(45°) = \frac{x - 2}{8}$$

$$1.0 = \frac{x - 2}{8}$$

$$8 = x - 2$$

$$10 = x$$

The flagpole is 10 meters high.

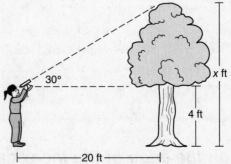

1. _____

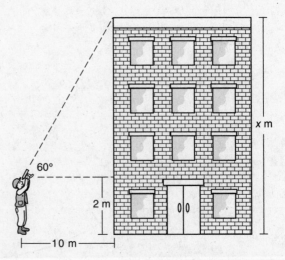

2. _____

Find the height of each of the following by using a calculator to find the approximate value of the tangent of the angle.

3. your school building _____

4. the flagpole _____

5. a tree _____

6. a telephone or an electric pole _____

7. the bleachers of the football field _____

8. another object

(name of object) _____ (height of object) _____

9. sporting equipment, such as the field goal post on the football field, a basketball hoop, or a soccer net

(name of equipment) _____ (height) _____

10. When would *you* use indirect measurement? _____

_____

_____

_____

_____

_____

_____

_____

_____

_____

Geometry Lab Recording Sheet

(Use with Extend 8-7 on page 601 in the Student Edition)

Adding Vectors

Materials: ruler

Exercises

Make a scale drawing to solve each problem.

1. **BIKING** Lance is riding his bike west at a velocity of 10 miles per hour. The wind is blowing 5 miles per hour 20° north of east. What is Lance's resultant velocity and direction?

2. **CANOEING** Bianca is trying to canoe directly across a river with a current of 3 miles per hour due west. If Bianca can canoe at a rate of 7 miles per hour, what is her resultant velocity and direction?

CHAPTER 9

Transformations and Symmetry
Teaching Notes and Overview

 Using Overhead Manipulatives

Constructing Reflections in a Line
(p. 122 of this booklet)

Use With Lesson 9–1.

Objective Create a reflection using dot paper.

Materials
dot paper transparency*
transparency pens*
straightedge
dot paper for students
* = available in Overhead Manipulative Resources

This demonstration involves using dot paper to create a reflection image. After you plot *J′*, you may wish to select students to come to the overhead and plot *K′*, *L′*, and *M′*.

In the extension, quadrilaterals *JKLM* and *J′K′L′M′* are reflected in a horizontal line. Students then work in pairs to complete reflections of images drawn by their partner on dot paper.

Answers
Answers appear on the teacher demonstration instructions on page 122.

 Using Overhead Manipulatives

Translations
(pp. 123–124 of this booklet)

Use With Lesson 9–2.

Objective Use translation images to draw a prism.

Materials
lined paper transparency*
regular polygons transparency*
coordinate grids transparency*

transparency pens*
straightedge
blank transparency
* = available in Overhead Manipulative Resources

This activity involves two demonstrations to draw a prism.

• Demonstration 1 uses the lined paper transparency and regular polygons transparency to draw a pentagonal prism. You may wish to have students follow along at their desks on a piece of lined paper. Ask students to explain how the pentagon was translated.

• Demonstration 2 uses the coordinate grids transparency to draw a triangular prism. Again, you may choose for students to follow along at their desks on a piece of grid paper.

• In this extension, students work in pairs to practice drawing translation images described by an ordered pair.

Answers
Answers appear on the teacher demonstration instructions on pages 123–124.

 Geometry Lab

Reflections and Translations
(pp. 125–126 of this booklet)

Use With Lesson 9–2.

Objective Use a geomirror to discover that two successive reflections in a pair of parallel lines is the same as a translation from the preimage.

Materials
classroom set of Geometry Lab worksheets
unlined paper
geomirror*
straightedge
* = available in Overhead Manipulative Resources

For this activity, students can work in groups of two or three. Before giving students the worksheets, you may wish to pass out and review how to use the geomirrors.

In this activity, students reflect and draw a figure in each of a pair of parallel lines. By examining the preimage and images, students make a conjecture that the resulting image from the pair of reflections is the same as translating the preimage.

Answers

1–5. See students' work.

6. The orientation remains unchanged.

7. yes

8. $AA'' = BB'' = CC'' = 2$(distance from ℓ to m)

9. Use a translation.

10. See students' work.

11. See students' work.

12. yes

Mini-Project

Graphing and Translations
(p. 127 of this booklet)

Use With Lesson 9–2.

Objective Perform translations and reflections of triangles and line segments.

For this activity, students should work in pairs. For Exercises 1 and 2, students graph triangles and their translated images. For Exercises 3 and 4, students draw line segments and their reflected images. Students should discover the relationship of the slope of a line segment and its image after a

reflection in the y-axis and then in the x-axis.

Answers

1.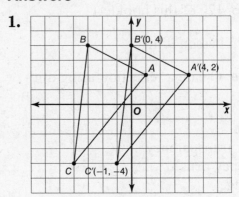

2.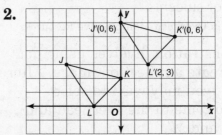

3.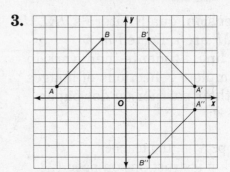

$(6, -1), (2, -5)$

4.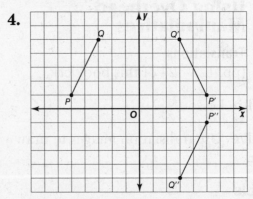

Slopes are $\overline{PQ}$: 2, $\overline{P'Q'}$: −2; $\overline{P''Q''}$: 2; the slopes of $\overline{PQ}$ and $\overline{P''Q''}$ are equal.

Geometry Lab Recording Sheet

Rotations
(pp. 128–129 of this booklet)

Use With Explore 9–3. This corresponds to the activity on page 631 in the Student Edition.

Objective Explore the properties of rotations.

Materials
patty paper

Students will use patty paper to rotate a quadrilateral. Then students will graph and rotate a triangle and make conjectures about rotations.

Answers
See Teacher Edition p. 631.

Using Overhead Manipulatives

Rotations
(pp. 130–131 of this booklet)

Use With Lesson 9–3.

Materials
straightedge
transparency pens*
blank transparencies
* = available in Overhead Manipulative Resources

This demonstration involves reflecting an image in a pair of intersecting lines to discover that this is the same as a rotation about the point of intersection of the two lines. You may wish to distribute patty paper or wax paper and have students complete the activity at their desks while you complete it at the overhead.

In this extension, students investigate the angle of rotation when an image is reflected in perpendicular lines.

Answers
Answers appear on the teacher demonstration instructions on pages 130–131.

Geometry Lab Recording Sheet

Tessellations
(pp. 132–134 of this booklet)

Use With Extend 9–4. This corresponds to the activity on pages 650–652 in the Student Edition.

Objective Identify regular tessellations. Create tessellations with and without technology.

Materials
none

In Activity 1, students will determine whether polygons will tessellate. In Activity 2, students will classify tessellations, and in Activity 3, they will draw a tessellation. Students will use their graphing calculators in Activity 4 to draw tessellations. Then students will practice what they have learned with tessellations in the exercises.

Answers
See Teacher Edition p. 652.

Using Overhead Manipulatives

(Use with Lesson 9-1)

Constructing Reflections in a Line

Objective Create a reflection using dot paper.

Materials
• dot paper transparency*
• transparency pens*
• straightedge
• dot paper for students
* = available in Overhead Manipulative Resources

Demonstration
Create a Reflection in a Vertical Line

• Draw the quadrilateral shown on the dot paper transparency. Use a colored transparency pen to draw a vertical line of reflection.

• Tell students that vertex *J* is 5 dots to the left of the line of reflection. Have students find a dot on the same row that is 5 dots to the right of the line of reflection. Label the dot *J'*.

• Repeat the steps for vertices *K, L,* and *M.* Draw lines between the vertices to complete the reflection.

• Have students compare the two figures. Ask them if the corresponding sides are congruent. **yes**

• Ask, "How is this reflection like a reflection in a mirror?" **Each point is the same distance from the line of reflection as its corresponding point. In a mirror, your reflection seems to be as far "into" the mirror as you are in front of the mirror.**

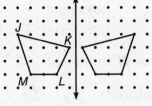

Extension
Create a Reflection in a Horizontal Line

• Add a horizontal line of reflection below the figures on the dot paper transparency. Reflect *JKLM* and *J'K"L'M"* in the horizontal line of reflection.

• Draw a triangle and a line of reflection that is neither vertical nor horizontal on the dot paper transparency. Have students draw the figure on dot paper. Students should work in pairs to complete the reflection.

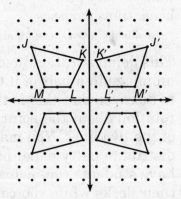

122

Teaching Geometry with Manipulatives

Using Overhead Manipulatives

(Use with Lesson 9-2)

Translations

Objective Use translation images to draw a prism.

Materials
- lined paper transparency*
- regular polygons transparency*
- coordinate grids transparency*
- transparency pens*
- straightedge
- blank transparency

* = available in Overhead Manipulative Resources

Demonstration 1
Draw a Prism Using a Translation Image

- Place the lined paper transparency over the regular polygons transparency and align the bottom of the pentagon with a line on the lined paper transparency. Trace the pentagon.

- Remove the regular polygons transparency. Lay a blank transparency over the lined paper transparency and trace the pentagon again.

- Slowly slide the blank transparency toward the upper right corner of the lined paper transparency. Stop when the bottom of the image pentagon is aligned with a different line of the lined paper.

- Use a straightedge to connect the corresponding vertices of the two pentagons. Make the segments representing sides of the solid that will be hidden from view dashed.

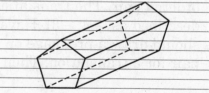

Demonstration 2
Draw a Prism Using a Translation Image

- Copy the graph below on the coordinate grids transparency.

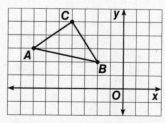

123

Using Overhead Manipulatives

- Lay a blank transparency over the coordinate grids transparency and copy the lines of △*ABC* onto the transparency with a transparency pen.

- Translate the image triangle 4 units to the left. Then translate the image 3 units down. Label the vertices of the image triangle *A'*, *B'*, and *C'*.

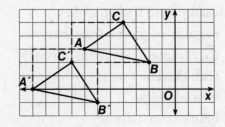

- Ask students to name the coordinates of the vertices of the image triangle. ***A'*(−11, 0), *B'*(−6, 21), *C'*(−8, 2)**

- Ask students to find the slope of the lines between *A*, *B*, and *C* and the corresponding vertices in the image triangle. **The slopes are all $\frac{3}{4}$.**

Extension
Describe Translations as Ordered Pairs

- Tell students that it is possible to describe a translation as an ordered pair. The translation from the demonstration can be described as (−4, −3). Have students work in pairs. Each student should draw a preimage on a coordinate grid and give an ordered pair for a translation. Then exchange papers and find the images.

NAME _____ DATE _____ PERIOD _____

Geometry Lab

(Use with Lesson 9-2)

Reflections and Translations

A geomirror is a construction instrument that allows you to find the reflection image of a figure. Use a geomirror with the following activity to investigate translations.

1. On a separate piece of paper, draw parallel lines ℓ and m, and triangle ABC.

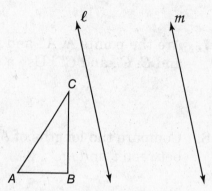

2. Place the geomirror so that the edge is aligned with line ℓ. Look into the geomirror to see the reflection image of $\triangle ABC$.

3. Use a straightedge to draw the image of $\triangle ABC$. Label the vertices A', B', and C'.

4. Align the edge of the geomirror with line m. Look into the geomirror to see the reflection image of $\triangle A'B'C'$.

5. Draw the image of $\triangle A'B'C'$. Label the vertices A'', B'', and C''.

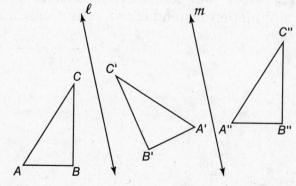

Refer to your drawing for Exercises 6–9.

6. You know that a reflection changes the orientation of its image. What happens when a figure is reflected twice?

7. Are the points A, A', and A'' collinear? How about B, B', and B'' and C, C', and C'''? Use a straightedge to verify your answer.

8. Compare the lengths of $\overline{AA''}$, $\overline{BB''}$ and $\overline{CC''}$, and the distance between ℓ and m.

9. Describe how you could map $\triangle ABC$ onto $\triangle A''B''C''$ in one motion instead of two reflections.

Use the geomirror to test whether two reflections will translate a regular polygon.

10. Draw two parallel lines and a regular polygon.

11. Reflect the regular polygon twice and compare the preimage and the image.

12. Does your conjecture in Exercise 9 about mapping in one motion instead of two reflections hold true?

Mini-Project

(Use with Lesson 9-2)

Graphing and Translations

Graph paper can help you draw transformation images of figures.

1. Graph $\triangle ABC$ with vertices $A(1, 2)$, $B(-3, 4)$, and $C(-4, -4)$. Draw $\triangle A'B'C'$, the translation image of $\triangle ABC$ where the distance of the slide is 3 units to the right. Name the coordinates of the translation image of each vertex.

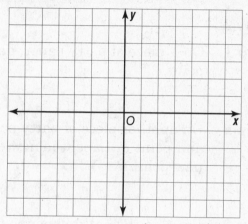

2. Draw $\triangle JKL$ with vertices $J(-4, 3)$, $K(0, 2)$, and $L(-2, 0)$. Let $\triangle J'K'L'$ be the image of $\triangle JKL$ under a slide of 4 units to the right followed by a slide of 3 units up. Graph $\triangle J'K'L'$. Name the coordinates of the vertices of $\triangle J'K'L'$.

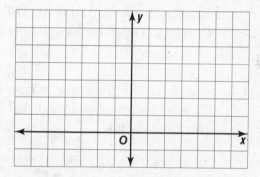

3. Draw $\overline{A'B'}$, the image formed by reflecting $\overline{AB}$ in the y-axis. Then draw $A''B''$, the image formed by reflecting $\overline{A'B'}$ in the x-axis. What are the coordinates of A'' and B''?

4. Draw $\overline{P'Q'}$, the reflection image of $\overline{PQ}$ in the y-axis. Draw $\overline{P''Q''}$, the reflection image of $\overline{P'Q'}$ in the x-axis. Find slopes of $\overline{PQ}$, $\overline{P'Q'}$, and $\overline{P''Q''}$. What is the relationship between the slopes of $\overline{PQ}$ and $\overline{P''Q''}$?

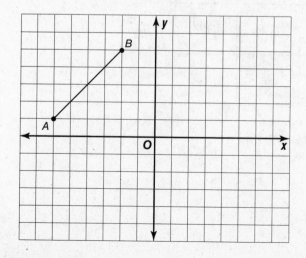

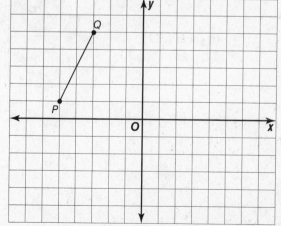

Geometry Lab Recording Sheet

(Use with Explore 9-3 on page 631 in the Student Edition)

Rotations

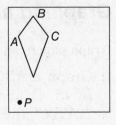

Materials: patty paper

Activity

Step 1 On a piece of patty paper, draw quadrilateral *ABCD* and point *P*.

Step 2 On another piece of patty paper, trace quadrilateral *ABCD* and point *P*. Label the new quadrilateral *A′B′C′D′* and the new point *P*.

Step 3 Position the patty paper so that both points *P* coincide. Rotate the paper so that *ABCD* and *A′B′C′D′* do not overlap. Tape the two pieces of patty paper together.

Step 4 Measure the distance between *A*, *B*, *C*, and *D* to point *P*. Repeat for quadrilateral *A′B′C′D′*. Then copy and complete the table below.

Quadrilateral	Length			
ABCD	AP	BP	CP	DP
A′B′C′D′	A′P	B′P	C′P	D′P

Exercises

1. Graph △*JKL* with vertices *J*(1, 3), *K*(2, 1), and *L*(3, 4) on a coordinate plane, and then trace on patty paper.

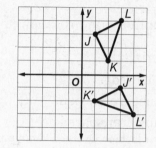

   a. Use a protractor to rotate each vertex 90° counterclockwise about the origin as shown in the figure at the right. What are the vertices of the rotated image?

   b. Rotate △*JKL* 180° about the origin. What are the vertices of the rotated image?

   c. Use the Distance Formula to find the distance from points *J*, *K*, and from *L* to the origin. Repeat for *J'K'L'* and *J"K"L"*.

2. ***Writing in Math*** If you rotate point (4, 2) 90° and 180° about the origin, how do the *x*- and *y*-coordinates change?

3. **MAKE A PREDICTION** What are the new coordinates of a point (*x*, *y*) that is rotated 270°?

4. **MAKE A CONJECTURE** Make a conjecture about the distances from the center of rotation *P* to each corresponding vertex of *ABCD* and *A'B'C'D'*.

Using Overhead Manipulatives

(Use with Lesson 9-3)

Rotations

Objective Find rotation images.

Materials
- straightedge
- transparency pens*
- blank transparencies

* = available in Overhead Manipulative Resources

Demonstration
Find Rotation Images about Intersecting Lines

- Use a blue transparency pen to draw a triangle and intersecting lines ℓ and m on a blank transparency. Label the point of intersection of lines ℓ and m as point A.

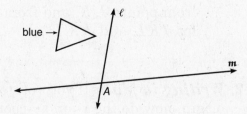

- Fold the transparency along line ℓ so that the side containing the triangle is on the bottom. Use a green transparency pen to trace the triangle. Unfold the transparency and ask students to describe the green triangle in terms of the blue triangle. **The green triangle is the reflection image of the blue triangle in line ℓ.**

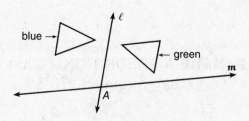

- Fold the transparency along line m so that the side containing the green triangle is on the bottom. Use a red transparency pen to trace the green triangle. Unfold the transparency and ask students to describe the red triangle in terms of the green triangle. **The red triangle is the reflection image of the green triangle in line m.**

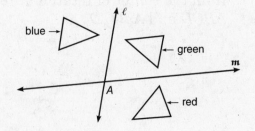

- Tell students that the red triangle is a composition of two reflections of the blue triangle in the intersecting lines.

• Place a second blank transparency over the diagram. Trace the blue triangle with a black transparency pen. Placing your pen point at point *A*, rotate the top transparency about point *A* until the black triangle coincides with the red triangle on the bottom transparency. Ask students to make a conjecture about the composition of reflections in two intersecting lines. **The image of two reflections in intersecting lines is the same as a rotation about the point of intersection of the two lines of reflection.**

Extension
Find Rotation Images about Perpendicular Lines

• Have students draw a preimage and two perpendicular lines *s* and *t*. Have them reflect the preimage in *s* and then in *t*. Then place a piece of unlined or waxed paper over the figure and trace the preimage. Rotate the preimage until it coincides with the image of the two reflections. Ask, "How many degrees must the paper be turned so the preimage and image coincide?" **180** Ask, "How is this related to the measure of the angle between the two lines of reflections?" **It is twice the measure of the angle between the lines of reflection.**

Geometry Lab Recording Sheet

(Use with Extend 9-4 on pages 650-652 in the Student Edition)

Tessellations

Materials: none

Activity 1

Determine whether each regular polygon will tessellate in a plane.
Explain.

a. hexagon

Let x represent the measure of an interior angle of a regular hexagon.

$x = \dfrac{180(n - 2)}{n}$ Interior Angle Formula

b. decagon

Let x represent the measure of an interior angle of a regular decagon.

$x = \dfrac{180(n - 2)}{n}$ Interior Angle Formula

Activity 2

Determine whether each pattern is a tessellation. If so, describe it as *regular*, *semi-regular*, or *neither* and *uniform* or *not uniform*.

a.

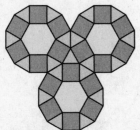

b.

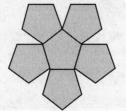

c.

Activity 3

Draw a triangle and use it to create a tessellation.

Step 1 Draw a triangle and find the midpoint of one side.

Step 2 Rotate the triangle 180° about the point.

Step 3 Translate the pair of triangles to make a row.

Step 4 Translate the row to make a tessellation.

Activity 4

Use Geometer's Sketchpad to create a tessellation.

Step 1 Insert three points and construct a line through two of the points. Then construct the line parallel to the first line through the thrid point using the **Parallel Line** option from the **Construct** menu. Complete the parallellogram and label the points *A*, *B*, *C*, and *D*. Hide the lines.

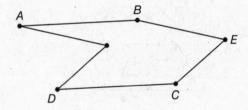

Step 2 Insert another point *E* on the exterior of the parallelogram. Draw the segments between *A* and *B*, *B* and *E*, *E* and *C*, and *C* and *D*.

Step 3 Highlight *B* and then *A*. From the **Transform** menu, choose **Mark Vector**. Select the $\overline{BE}$, $\overline{EC}$, and point *E*. From the **Transform** menu, choose **Translate**.

Step 4 Starting with *A*, Select all of the vertices around the perimeter of the polygon. Choose **Hexagon Interior** from the **Construct** menu.

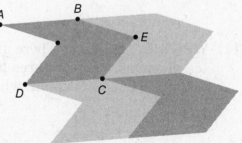

Step 5 Choose point *A* and then point *B* and mark the vector as you did in Step 3. Select the interior of the polygon and choose **Translate** from the **Transform** menu. Continue the tessellations by marking vectors and translating the polygon. You can choose **Color** from the **Display** menu to create a color pattern.

Exercises

Determine whether each regular polygon will tessellate in the plane. Write *yes* or *no*. Explain.

1. triangle

2. pentagon

3. 16-gon

Determine whether each pattern is a tessellation. Write *yes* or *no*. If so, describe it as *regular*, *semi-regular*, or *neither* and *uniform* or *not uniform*.

4.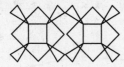

5.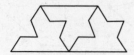

6.

Draw a tessellation using the following shape(s).

7. octagon and square

8. hexagon and triangle

9. right triangle

10. trapezoid and a parallelogram

11. **WRITING IN MATH** There are only three possible regular tessellations. List the three polygons used to create these tessellations, and explain why they are the only ones possible.

12. **MAKE A CONJECTURE** Describe a figure that you think will tessellate in three-dimensional space. Explain your reasoning.

CHAPTER 10 Circles
Teaching Notes and Overview

Using Overhead Manipulatives

Locating the Center of a Circle
(p. 138 of this booklet)

Use With Lesson 10-3.

Objective Use constructions to find the center of a circle.

Materials
compass*
straightedge
transparency pens*
blank transparency
* = available in Overhead Manipulative Resources

This demonstration involves constructing and investigating the intersection of the perpendicular bisectors of two nonparallel chords of a circle.

In the extension, students discuss other methods to finding the center of a circle.

Answers
Answers appear on the teacher demonstration instructions on page 138.

Mini-Project

More About Circles
(p. 139 of this booklet)

Use With Lesson 10-3.

Objective Use circles and paper folding to discover characteristics and properties of chords.

Materials
unlined paper
compass*
ruler*
scissors*
* = available in Overhead Manipulative Resources

Students discover that they can use parallel and nonparallel chords to locate the center of a circle.

Answers

1. octagon **2.** hexagon **3.** See students' work.

4. Yes; the perpendicular bisectors are the same segment. Extend this segment until it becomes a diameter, then bisect it.

Using Overhead Manipulatives

Investigating Inscribed Angles
(p. 140 of this booklet)

Use With Lesson 10-4.

Objective Investigate the measure of an angle inscribed in a circle.

Materials
compass*
protractor*
straightedge
transparency pens*
blank transparency
* = available in Overhead Manipulative Resources

This demonstration involves drawing a central angle and several inscribed angles that intercept the same arc to discover the relationship among these two types of angles. While students are examining circles of different sizes at their desks, encourage them to draw central angles of various sizes.

Answers
Answers appear on the teacher demonstration instructions on page 140.

Geometry Lab

Inscribed Angles
(pp. 141–143 of this booklet)

Use With Lesson 10-4.

Objective Define and measure inscribed and central angles of a circle.

Materials
classroom set of Geometry Lab worksheets
transparency master of Geometry Lab
blank transparencies

Display the transparency master on the overhead. Ask students to find how many degrees there are from one dot on the circle to the next. Use a blank transparency to draw a central angle on the circular grid. Ask students to find the measure of the central angle.

Answers

1a. 30   **1b.** 90   **1c.** 150

1d. 150   **2a.** 75, 75   **2b.** 45, 45

2c. 15, 15   **2d.** 15, 15

3. 30, 120, 150; They are equal.

4. They are congruent; answers may vary.

5. See students' angles.

6a. 45, 75, 60, 180

6b. 90, 90, 90, 90, 360

6c. 127.5, 127.5, 90, 82.5, 112.5, 540

6d. 120, 120, 120, 120, 120, 120, 720

7. Yes; sum of measures of angles = $(n - 2)180$, where n = number of sides

Using Overhead Manipulatives

Constructing a Circle to Inscribe a Triangle
(p. 144 of this booklet)

Use With Lesson 10-4.

Objective Construct a circle so that a given triangle is inscribed in it.

Materials
compass*
straightedge
transparency pens*
blank transparencies
* = available in Overhead Manipulative Resources

This demonstration involves constructing a circle that inscribes a triangle. After drawing $\triangle RST$, you may wish to ask students for suggestions on how to construct a circle that will inscribe the triangle.

In this extension, students work in pairs to explore the types of polygons (regular, convex, and concave) that can be inscribed in a circle. You may wish to select a few students to demonstrate at the overhead how to inscribe a polygon, other than a triangle, in a circle.

Answers
Answers appear on the teacher demonstration instructions on page 144.

Using Overhead Manipulatives

Constructing Tangents
(pp. 145–146 of this booklet)

Use With Lesson 10-5.

Objective Construct a tangent to a circle through a point on or outside of the circle.

Materials
compass*
straightedge
transparency pens*
blank transparency
* = available in Overhead Manipulative Resources

This activity includes two demonstrations on constructing tangents to a circle. You may need to review with students how to construct perpendicular lines through a point on the line and through a point not on the line.

Answers
Answers appear on the teacher demonstration instructions on pages 145-146.

Using Overhead Manipulatives

Inscribing a Circle in a Triangle
(p. 147 of this booklet)

Use With Lesson 10-5.

Objective Inscribe a circle in a given triangle.

Materials
compass*
straightedge
transparency pens*
blank transparencies
* = available in Overhead Manipulative Resources

This demonstration involves constructing a circle that is inscribed in a triangle.

In this extension, students prove that a circle can be inscribed in any triangle. Before determining how to prove this, you may encourage students to complete the construction at their desk with a triangle of any size.

Answers
Answers appear on the teacher demonstration instructions on page 147.

Geometry Lab Recording Sheet

Inscribed and Circumscribed Triangles
(pp. 148–149 of this booklet)

Use With Extend 10-5. This corresponds to the activity on pages 726 in the Student Edition.

Objective Construct inscribed circles and circumscribed triangles.

Materials
compass*
straightedge
* = available in Overhead Manipulative Resources

In this activity, students learn how to construct a circle inscribed in a triangle and a circle circumscribed about a triangle.

Answers
See Teacher Edition page 726.

Using Overhead Manipulatives

(Use with Lesson 10-3)

Locating the Center of a Circle

> **Objective** Use construction to find the center of a circle.
>
> **Materials**
> - compass*
> - straightedge
> - transparency pens*
> - blank transparency
>
> * = available in Overhead Manipulative Resource

Demonstration
Locate the Center of a Circle

- Use the compass to draw any circle on a blank transparency. Then, draw any two nonparallel chords. Label the chords $\overline{TU}$ and $\overline{VW}$.

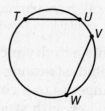

- Construct the perpendicular bisector of each chord. Call them, ℓ and m. Label the intersection of, ℓ and m point X.

- Ask students to explain why we can claim that X is the center of the circle. **ℓ and m contain diameters of the circle since the perpendicular bisector of a chord must be a diameter. The only point two diameters of a circle share is the center of the circle.**

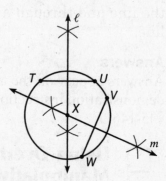

Extension
More Ways to Locate the Center of a Circle

- Divide students into groups of three or four. Have students work together to discover as many ways of finding the center of a circle as they can. Encourage students to use paper folding, construction, or another technique. Ask a representative from each group to demonstrate and justify one of their methods for finding the center.

Mini-Project

(Use with Lesson 10-3)

More About Circles

1. Complete each of the following steps.

   a. Draw a circle with a 4-inch radius and cut it out.

   b. Fold the circle in half.

   c. Fold the circle in half again.

   d. Fold the circle in half one more time.

   e. Unfold the circle and draw a chord between each of the adjacent endpoints created by the folds.

   What figure have you drawn?

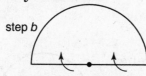 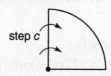

2. Complete each of the following steps.

   a. Draw another 4-inch radius circle and cut it out.

   b. Fold the circle in half.

   c. Fold the two sides so they meet in the middle as shown.

   d. Unfold the circle and draw a chord between each of the adjacent endpoints created by the folds.

   What figure have you drawn?

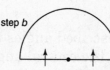 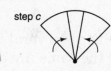

3. In a circle, the perpendicular bisector of any chord passes through the center of the circle. If you choose any two chords that are not parallel, then the intersection of their perpendicular bisectors must be the center of the circle. Use this fact to find the center of each of the following circles.

   a. 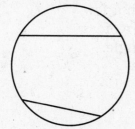   **b.** 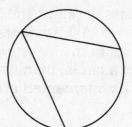   **c.**

4. Draw a circle. Draw two chords that are parallel. Using those two chords, can you find the center of the circle?

Teaching Geometry with Manipulatives

Using Overhead Manipulatives

(Use with Lesson 10-4)

Investigating Inscribed Angles

Objective Investigate the measure of an angle inscribed in a circle.

Materials
• compass*
• protractor*
• straightedge
• transparency pens*
• blank transparency
* = available in Overhead Manipulative Resources

Demonstration
Investigate Inscribed Angles

• Draw a large circle C on a blank transparency. Using a straightedge, draw a central angle. Find the measure of the central angle with a protractor and record the measure on the transparency.

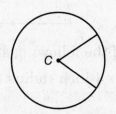

$m\angle C = 68$

• Draw several inscribed angles that intercept the same arc as the central angle. Have students measure each inscribed angle and record these measures on the transparency.

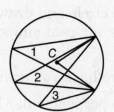

$m\angle C = 68$
$m\angle 1 = 34$
$m\angle 2 = 34$
$m\angle 3 = 34$

• Have students work in pairs to repeat the investigation with a few more circles of different sizes. Ask students how the measure of each inscribed angle relates to the measure of the central angle. **If an angle is inscribed in a circle, then its measure equals one-half the measure of its intercepted arc.**

NAME _____ DATE _____ PERIOD _____

Geometry Lab

(Use with Lesson 10-4)

Inscribed Angles

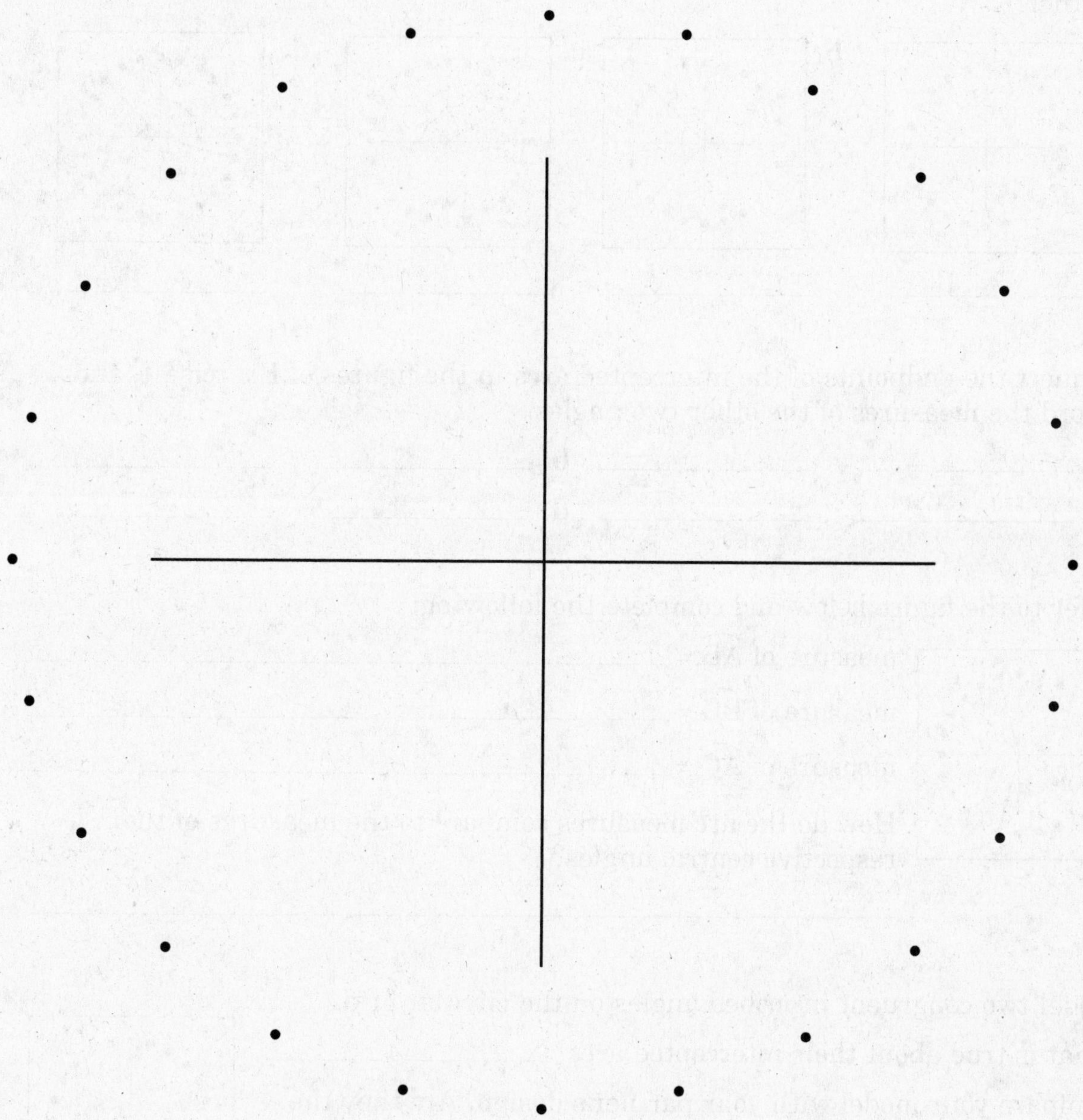

141

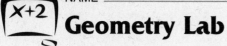

Geometry Lab

(Use with Lesson 10-4)

Inscribed Angles

1. Discuss the measures of the central angles in the figures below with your partner.

a. 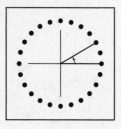   **b.** 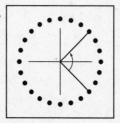   **c.** 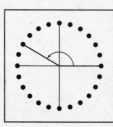   **d.**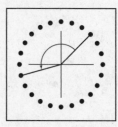

_____   _____   _____   _____

2. Connect the endpoints of the intercepted arcs in the figures of Exercise 1, and record the measures of the other two angles.

a. _____   _____   **b.** _____   _____

c. _____   _____   **d.** _____   _____

3. Refer to the figure below and complete the following:

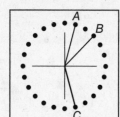

measure of $\overset{\frown}{AB}$ = _____

measure of $\overset{\frown}{BC}$ = _____

measure of $\overset{\frown}{AC}$ = _____

How do the arc measures compare to the measures of their respective central angles?

_____

_____

4. Model two congruent inscribed angles on the circular grid.

What is true about their intercepted arcs? _____

Compare your model with your partner's design. Are they the same?

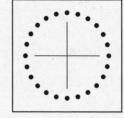

_____

List possible conclusions from your models. _____

_____

5. On the circular grids draw inscribed angles measuring 45°, 30°, 60°, 90°, and 120°.

45°   30°   60°   90°   120°

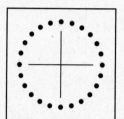 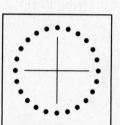 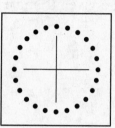 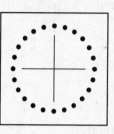 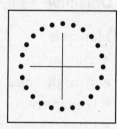

6. Record the measures of the angles in each figure below.

a.   **b.**   **c.**   **d.**

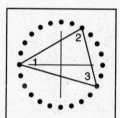 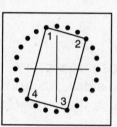 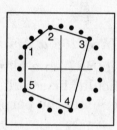 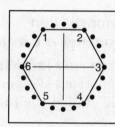

$m\angle 1$ _____	$m\angle 1$ _____	$m\angle 1$ _____	$m\angle 1$ _____
$m\angle 2$ _____	$m\angle 2$ _____	$m\angle 2$ _____	$m\angle 2$ _____
$m\angle 3$ _____	$m\angle 3$ _____	$m\angle 3$ _____	$m\angle 3$ _____
Total = _____	$m\angle 4$ _____	$m\angle 4$ _____	$m\angle 4$ _____
	Total = _____	$m\angle 5$ _____	$m\angle 5$ _____
		Total = _____	$m\angle 6$ _____
			Total = _____

7. Can you find a pattern from the totals in Exercise 6?

_____

What conclusions can you make about the sum of the measures of the interior angles of an inscribed polygon?

_____

Using Overhead Manipulatives

(Use with Lesson 10-5)

Constructing a Circle to Inscribe a Triangle

Objective Construct a circle so that a given triangle is inscribed in it.

Materials
- compass*
- straightedge
- transparency pens*
- blank transparencies

* = available in Overhead Manipulative Resources

Demonstration
Construct a Circle to Inscribe a Triangle

- Draw any large triangle RST on a blank transparency. Construct the perpendicular bisectors for two sides, $\overline{RS}$ and $\overline{ST}$. Label the intersection of the perpendicular bisectors C.

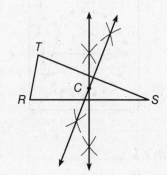

- Using C as a center, and CR as the measure of the radius, draw $\odot C$. Then $\triangle RST$ is inscribed in $\odot C$.

- Ask students "What kind of segments in a circle do the sides of $\triangle RST$ represent?" **chords** Ask students to explain why the construction works. **The perpendicular bisector of a chord of a circle contains a diameter of the circle, so the perpendicular bisectors of $\overline{RS}$ and $\overline{ST}$ contain diameters of a circle in which $\overline{RS}$ and $\overline{ST}$ are chords.**

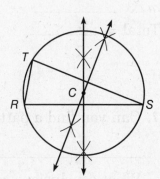

Extension
Investigate Polygons that can be Inscribed in a Circle

- Explain that not all polygons can be inscribed in a circle. Have students work in pairs to investigate which polygons cannot be inscribed in a circle. Suggest that students organize their investigation by making a table listing all of the different types of polygons with up to eight sides that they can think of. Include regular, convex, and concave polygons. Then use the table to record which types of polygons can or cannot be inscribed in a circle. **Concave polygons cannot be inscribed in a circle.**

Using Overhead Manipulatives
(Use with Lesson 10-5)

Constructing Tangents

Objective Construct a tangent to a circle through a point on or outside of the circle.

Materials
- compass*
- straightedge
- transparency pens*
- blank transparencies

* = available in Overhead Manipulative Resources

Demonstration 1
Construct a Tangent through a Point on a Circle

- Use a compass to draw a circle C. Choose a point on the circle and label it D. Draw $\overrightarrow{CD}$.

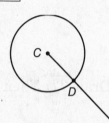

- Construct line ℓ, through D and perpendicular to $\overrightarrow{CD}$. You may wish to refer students to the construction of a perpendicular line through a point on the line in Lesson 1-5 of *Geometry*.

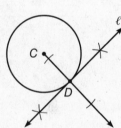

- Ask students to explain why ℓ is tangent to $\odot C$ at D. **ℓ is perpendicular to radius $\overrightarrow{CD}$ at its endpoint, D, on the circle, so line ℓ is tangent to $\odot C$.**

Demonstration 2
Construct a Tangent through a Point Not on a Circle

- Use a compass to draw a circle S. Choose a point outside of the circle and label it T. Draw $\overrightarrow{TS}$.

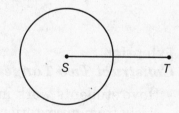

145

Teaching Geometry with Manipulatives

- Construct the perpendicular bisector of $\overline{TS}$. Call this line ℓ. Label the intersection of ℓ and $\overline{TS}$ point R.

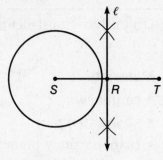

- Using R as the center, draw a circle with radius measuring RS. Call U and V the intersection points of the two circles.

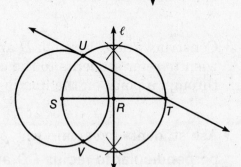

- Draw $\overleftrightarrow{TU}$ Then $\overleftrightarrow{TU}$ is tangent to $\odot S$.

- Point out that $\overleftrightarrow{TU}$ is tangent to $\odot S$ if $\overleftrightarrow{TU} \perp \overline{US}$. Ask, "How do you know that $\angle SUT$ is a right angle?" **It is inscribed in a semicircle.**

Extension
Construct Two Tangents from an Exterior Point

- Have students work in pairs to construct the two tangents to a circle from an exterior point. Have them repeat the construction and measure each of the segments from the exterior point to the point of tangency. Ask students to make a conjecture about the measures of two tangent segments from an exterior point. **The two tangent segments from an exterior point to a circle are congruent.**

NAME _____ DATE _____ PERIOD _____

Using Overhead Manipulatives

(Use with Lesson 10-5)

Inscribing a Circle in a Triangle

Objective Inscribe a circle in a given triangle.

Materials
- compass*
- straightedge
- transparency pens*
- blank transparencies

* = available in Overhead Manipulative Resources

Demonstration
Inscribe a Circle in a Triangle

- Draw a large triangle on a blank transparency. Label it $\triangle LMN$. Construct the angle bisector of $\angle L$ and $\angle N$. You may wish to refer students to the construction of an angle bisector in Lesson 1-4 of *Glencoe Geometry*. Extend the bisectors to intersect at point P.

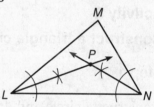

- Construct a line from P perpendicular to $\overline{LN}$. Label the intersection of the perpendicular line and $\overline{LN}$ as point Q.

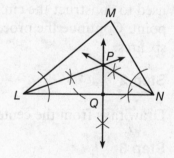

- Set the compass length equal to PQ and draw $\odot P$.

- Ask students to explain why the construction works. **Every point on the bisector of an angle is equidistant from the sides of the angle, so the intersection of the bisectors is equidistant from all three sides of the triangle. Therefore, a circle drawn with the intersection point as the center and the distance from the point to one of the sides as the measure of the radius will be tangent to all three sides.**

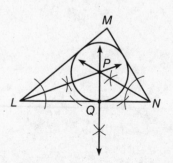

Extension
Inscribe a Circle in Any Triangle

- Have students work in pairs to prove that a circle can be inscribed in any triangle.

Geometry Lab Recording Sheet
(Use with Extend 10-5 on pages 726 in the Student Edition)

Inscribed and Circumscribed Circles

Materials: compass, straightedge

Activity 1

Construct a circle inscribed in a triangle.

Step 1 Draw a triangle *XYZ*, and construct two angle bisectors of the triangle to locate the incenter *W*.

Step 2 Construct a segment perpendicular to a side through the incenter. Label the intersection *R*.

Step 3 Set a compass of the length of $\overline{WR}$. Put the point of the compass on *W* and draw a circle with that radius.

Activity 2

Construct a triangle circumscribed about a circle.

Step 1

Construct a circle and draw a point. Use the same compass setting you used to construct the circle to construct an arc on the circle from the point. Continue the process from the previous arc until you have drawn six arcs.

Step 2

Draw rays from the center through every other arc.

Step 3

Construct a line perpendicular to each of the rays.

Model and Analyze

1. In Activity 1, why is it only necessary to construct the perpendicular to one side of the triangle?

2. Draw a right triangle and inscribe a circle in it.

3. **CHALLENGE** Circumscribe an obtuse triangle about a circle. Explain your reasoning.

4. *Writing in Math* Why do you think the term *incenter* is a good term for the point it defines?

149

CHAPTER 11

Areas of Polygons and Circles
Teaching Notes and Overview

Using Overhead Manipulatives

Investigating the Area of a Trapezoid
(pp. 153–154 of this booklet)

Use With Lesson 11-2.

Objective Derive the formula for the area of a trapezoid.

Materials
straightedge
centimeter grid transparency*
lined paper transparency*
transparency pens*
centimeter grid paper
scissors*
tape
* = available in Overhead Manipulative Resources

In this demonstration, students discover the similarities and differences between the area formulas for a parallelogram and a trapezoid. Through the students' knowledge of the formula for the area of a parallelogram, they can develop the formula for the area of a trapezoid.

In the extension, students repeat the activity with two different trapezoids. Ask students whether this activity will work with a trapezoid of any size. Have them explain their reasoning.

Answers
Answers appear on the teacher demonstration instructions on pages 153–154.

Geometry Lab Recording Sheet

Real Estate Property Values
(p. 155 of this booklet)

Use With Extend 11-2. This corresponds to the activity on page 781 in the Student Edition.

Objective Use a spreadsheet to organize and compare descriptive data.

Materials
spreadsheet software

Students will use spreadsheets to find the highest and lowest selling price of a house.

Answers
See Teacher Edition p. 781.

Mini-Project

Areas of Circular Regions
(pp. 156–157 of this booklet)

Use With Lesson 11-3.

Objective Find the area of the space that the dog can reach while on a 12-foot chain.

Materials
compass

For this activity, students should work in pairs. Students should first use a compass to draw the circular region in each figure with the radius defined by the segment labeled "12 ft." Then students will use the formula for the area of a circle to calculate the space in each figure that Rover can reach while on the 12-foot chain. Remind students that each circular region, except in Exercise 1, is only a portion of a circle.

Answers

1. 452.4 ft^2
2. 226.2 ft^2
3. 339.3 ft^2
4. 389.6 ft^2

Geometry Lab Recording Sheet

Investigating Areas of Regular Polygons
(p. 158 of this booklet)

Use With Explore 11-4. This corresponds to the activity on page 790 in the Student Edition.

Objective Investigate the formula for the area of regular polygons.

Materials
straightedge
protractor

Students will construct an apothem of a regular pentagon and use its measure to calculate the pentagon's area.

Answers
See Teacher Edition p. 790.

Using Overhead Manipulatives

Constructing a Regular Hexagon
(p. 159 of this booklet)

Use With Lesson 11-4.

Objective Construct a regular hexagon.

Materials
straightedge
compass*
transparency pens*
blank transparency
* = available in Overhead Manipulative Resources

This demonstration involves using a compass and straightedge to construct a regular hexagon. Since students will use hexagon *HIJKLM* for the extension, you may wish to have the students complete the construction of the

hexagon at their desks while you complete the construction at the overhead.

In the extension, students work in pairs to construct an apothem of hexagon *HIJKLM*.

Answers
Answers appear on the teacher demonstration instructions on page 176.

Geometry Lab

Area of a Regular Polygon
(pp. 160–161 of this booklet)

Use With Lesson 11-4.

Objective Derive the area formula for a regular polygon.

Materials
classroom set of Geometry Lab worksheets
scissors*
straightedge
* = available in Overhead Manipulative Resources

In this activity, students use a regular hexagon inscribed in a circle to derive the formula for the area of a regular polygon. Throughout the activity, you may wish to assess the students' progress by checking their answers to Exercises 7, 10, and 18. The formula for the area of a regular polygon is derived by examining the area of the hexagon in relation to the area of the triangles that compose the hexagon. Once students complete the activity, you may wish to have them repeat the process with another regular polygon.

Answers

1–5. See students' work.

6. radii

7. $p = AB + BC + CD + DE + EF + FA$

8. 6

9. They are congruent.

10. The area of the hexagon equals the sum of the areas of the triangles.
area of $ABCDE$ = area of $\triangle AOB$ + area of $\triangle BOC$ + area of $\triangle COD$ + area of $\triangle DOE$ area of $\triangle EOF$ + area of $\triangle FOA$

11. See students' work.

12. They are perpendicular.

13. the height

14. $\frac{1}{2}aDE$

15. yes

16. They are equal.

17a. $\frac{1}{2}aCD$

17b. $\frac{1}{2}aBC$

17c. $\frac{1}{2}aAB$

17d. $\frac{1}{2}aAF$

17e. $\frac{1}{2}aEF$

18. area of hexagon $ABCDEF$
$$= \frac{1}{2}a(DE) + \frac{1}{2}a(CD) + \frac{1}{2}a(BC) + \frac{1}{2}a(AB) + \frac{1}{2}a(AF) + \frac{1}{2}a(EF)$$

19. area of hexagon $ABCDEF = \frac{1}{2}$
$a(DE + CD + BC + AB + AF + EF)$

20. area of hexagon $ABCDEF = \frac{1}{2}ap$

21. Sample answer: A regular polygon can be separated into congruent nonoverlapping triangles. The sum of the areas of the triangles is the area of the polygon. The area of one triangle is $\frac{1}{2}$ times the product of the base and the height. The base of the triangle is the length of one side of the polygon and the height is the apothem of the polygon. This can be rewritten as $\frac{1}{2}sa$. The area of a regular polygon is $\frac{1}{2}Pa$ where P is the perimeter of the polygon or the sum of the sides, s, of each triangle.

Geometry Lab Recording Sheet

Areas of Irregular Figures
(pp. 162–163 of this booklet)

Use With Extend 11-4. This corresponds to the activity on pages 800–801 in the Student Edition.

Objective Estimate the areas of irregular polygons.

Materials
grid paper

Students will use different techniques to find the area of irregular figures.

Answers

See Teacher Edition pp. 800–801.

Using Overhead Manipulatives

(Use with Lesson 11-2)

Investigating the Area of a Trapezoid

Objective Find the area of a trapezoid, and develop a formula for the area of a trapezoid.

Materials
- straightedge
- centimeter grid transparency*
- lined paper transparency*
- transparency pens*
- centimeter grid paper
- scissors*
- tape

* = available in Overhead Manipulative Resources

Demonstration
Investigate the Area of a Trapezoid

- Review the definition of a trapezoid. Ask students how a parallelogram and a trapezoid are the same and how they are different. **They are both quadrilaterals, but a parallelogram has two pairs of sides parallel and a trapezoid has only one pair of sides parallel.**

- Ask students if the formula for the area of a parallelogram can be used to find the area of a trapezoid. Explain. **No, the bases of a trapezoid are not the same measure.**

- On the centimeter grid transparency, draw a trapezoid with bases 14 centimeters and 18 centimeters long and with a height of 8 centimeters. Label the bases and height as shown. Record the measures of the bases and the height in a chart on the lined paper transparency.

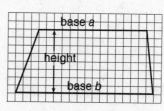

- Draw an identical trapezoid on centimeter grid paper. Cut out the trapezoid. Show students that it is the same size and shape as the trapezoid drawn on the transparency.

- Fold the paper trapezoid so that the bases align. Unfold and cut the paper trapezoid along the fold.

- Place the pieces together to form a parallelogram. Tape the pieces together and place on the centimeter grid transparency.

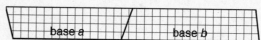

- Ask students to find the length of the base of the parallelogram. **32 cm** Ask them how it compares with the measures of the bases of the trapezoid. **It is the sum of the measures of the bases of the trapezoid.**

- Ask students to find the height of the parallelogram. **4 cm** Ask them how it compares with the height of the trapezoid. **It is half of the height of the trapezoid.**

- Ask students to find the area of the parallelogram. **128 cm²**

- Ask students what the area of the trapezoid is. **It is the same as the area of the parallelogram, 128 cm².**

- Ask students to write a formula for the area of any trapezoid. $A = \frac{1}{2}h(b_1 + b_2)$

Extension

Use the Area Formula for a Trapezoid

- Have students repeat the activity to find the area of each trapezoid described below.
  - bases: 13 centimeters and 17 centimeters; height: 16 centimeters **240 cm²**
  - bases: 5 centimeters and 15 centimeters; height: 14 centimeters **140 cm²**

Geometry Lab Recording Sheet

(Use with Extend 11-2 on page 781 in the Student Edition)

Real Estate Property Values

Materials: spreadsheet software

Activity 1

Design a spreadsheet to compare the houses using the information given.

Real Estate Property Values					
A	B	C	D	E	F
		House A	House B	House C	House D
2 Properly Condition					
3 Year Built					
4 Square Feet					
5 Bedrooms					
6 Baths					
7 Garage					
8 Lot size					
9 Basement					

Sheet 1 / Sheet 2 / Sheet 3

Model and Analyze

1. Fill in the spreadsheet using the descriptions of Houses A-D.

2. **MAKE A CONJECTURE** Which house do you think would have the highest selling price? the lowest selling price? Explain.

3. *Writing in Math* Write a description of another house that would be similar to the listed houses. Add the data to the table.

Mini-Project

(Use with Lesson 11-3)

Areas of Circular Regions

Robin is going to fix a chain to tie up his dog Rover. There are several places in the yard that Robin can attach the end of the chain. For each of the following, use a compass to draw the space that Rover can reach while on the end of a 12-foot chain. Then find the area. Round to the nearest tenth.

1. Rover's chain is attached to a stake in the middle of the yard.

12 ft

2. Rover's chain is attached to a long wall.

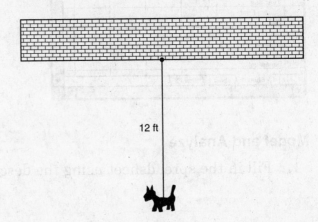

12 ft

3. Rover's chain is attached to the corner of the house.

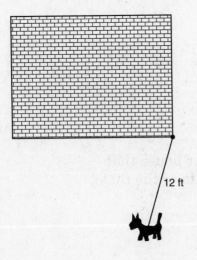

12 ft

4. Rover's chain is attached to a 4-foot by 18-foot rectangular shed.

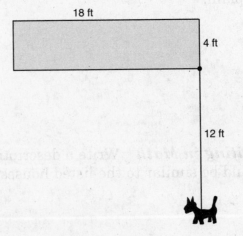

18 ft

4 ft

12 ft

14. What is the area of $\triangle EOD$?

15. Do all six triangles have an apothem?

16. How are the apothems of all six triangles related?

17. Find the area of each triangle. (Hint: Let a represent the height of each triangle.)

    a. $\triangle DOC$ **b.** $\triangle COB$ **c.** $\triangle BOA$

    d. $\triangle AOF$ **e.** $\triangle FOE$

18. Refer back to the equation you wrote in Exercise 10. Use substitution and the equations from Exercises 14 and 17 to write a new equation for the area of hexagon *ABCDEF*.

19. Use the distributive property and factor out the common factor of the equation in Exercise 18.

20. Refer back to the equation you wrote in Exercise 7. Use substitution to write a simplified equation for the area of hexagon *ABCDEF*.

21. Write a summary as to how you can use this method to prove that $A = \frac{1}{2}Pa$ is the area formula for any regular polygon.

Geometry Lab Recording Sheet

(Use with Explore 11-3 on page 790 in the Student Edition)

Investigating Areas of Regular Polygons

Materials
straightedge
protractor

Activity
Use the regular pentagon *ABCDE* shown for Steps 1–7.

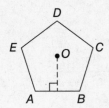

Analyze the Results

1. The area of a pentagon *ABCDE* can be found by adding the areas of the given triangles that make up the pentagonal region.

   $$A = \frac{1}{2}sa + \frac{1}{2}sa + \frac{1}{2}sa + \frac{1}{2}sa + \frac{1}{2}sa$$

   $$A = \frac{1}{2}(sa + sa + sa + sa + sa) \text{ or } \frac{1}{2}(5sa)$$

   What does 5*s* represent?

2. Write a formula for the area of a pentagon in terms of perimeter *P*.

Using Overhead Manipulatives

(Use with Lesson 11-4)

Constructing a Regular Hexagon

Objective Construct a regular hexagon.

Materials
- straightedge
- compass*
- transparency pens*
- blank transparency

* = available in Overhead Manipulative Resources

Demonstration
Construct a Regular Hexagon

- Draw a circle with the compass. Choose a point on the circle and label it *H*.

- With the same compass setting, place the compass on point *H*. Draw a small arc that intersects the circle. Label the point of intersection with the circle point *I*. Place the compass on point *I*. Draw another small arc that intersects the circle. Label that intersection point *J*. Continue this process, labeling points *K*, *L*, and *M*, until you come back to point *H*.

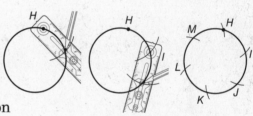

- Use a straightedge to connect the points *H, I, J, K, L*, and *M* in order. Ask students what is true about all of the segments. **They are congruent.**

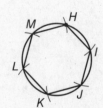

- Ask students if this is a regular hexagon. **yes**

Extension
Construct an Apothem of a Regular Hexagon

- Explain that an apothem is a segment drawn from the center of a regular polygon perpendicular to a side of the polygon. Ask students to work in pairs to construct an apothem of hexagon *HIJKLM*. **Construct a line through *C* perpendicular to $\overline{HI}$.**

Geometry Lab

(Use with Lesson 11-4)

Area of a Regular Polygon

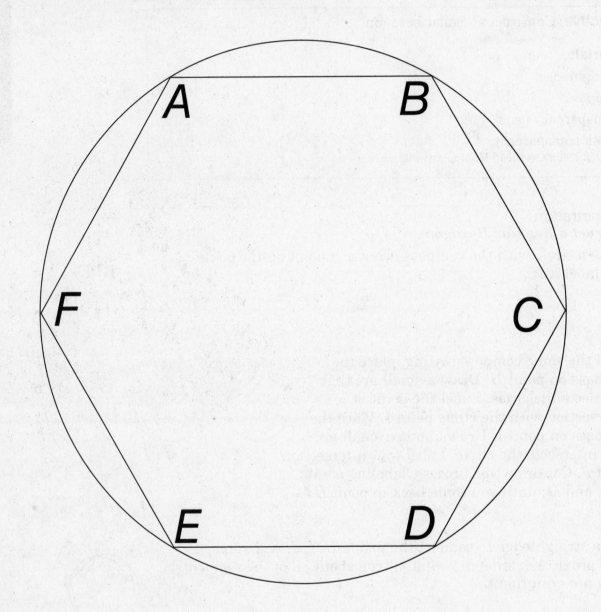

1. Cut out the circle circumscribed around hexagon *ABCDEF*.

2. Fold $\overline{AB}$ on $\overline{ED}$ and crease through *F* and *C*.

3. Open the circle and fold $\overline{BC}$ on $\overline{FE}$ and crease through *A* and *D*.

4. Open the circle and fold $\overline{CD}$ on $\overline{AF}$ and crease through *B* and *E*.

5. Draw $\overline{AD}$, $\overline{BE}$, and $\overline{CF}$ formed by the folds. Call the point where all the segments intersect, point *O*.

6. Consider circle *O*. What can you call $\overline{OA}$, $\overline{OB}$, $\overline{OC}$, $\overline{OD}$, $\overline{OE}$, and $\overline{OF}$?

7. Write an equation for the perimeter of hexagon *ABCDEF*.

8. How many triangles are formed by all the segments and all the sides of hexagon *ABCDEF*?

9. How are the triangles related?

10. How is the area of the hexagon related to the areas of the triangles? Write an equation to represent this.

11. Fold $\overline{ED}$ on itself and crease so that the crease passes through *O*. Label the intersection of $\overline{ED}$ and the crease point *L*. Let $\overline{OL}$ represent the apothem, *a*, of the polygon.

12. How are *a* and $\overline{ED}$ related?

13. Consider $\triangle \overline{EOD}$. What is *a* in $\triangle EOD$?

Geometry Lab Recording Sheet

(Use with Extend 11-4 on pages 800-801 in the Student Edition)

Areas of Irregular Figures

Materials: grid paper

Activity 1

Estimate the area of the figure.

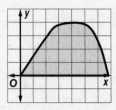

Step 1 Separate the irregular figure into rectangles of equal width.

Step 2 Find the area of each rectangle.

Step 3 Add all of the areas of the rectangles.

Activity 2

Estimate the area of the figure.

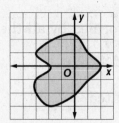

Step 1 Count the number of whole and partial squares inside the figure.

Step 2 Add the number of whole and partial squares.

Activity 3

Estimate the area of the figure.

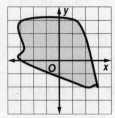

Step 1   Draw a rectangle around the irregular figure.

Step 2   Find the area of the rectangle.

Step 3   Find the areas of the unshaded triangles.

Step 4   Subtract the areas of the triangles from the area of the rectangle.

Exercises

Estimate the area of each irregular figure.

1.

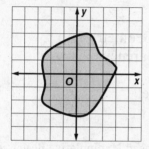

2.

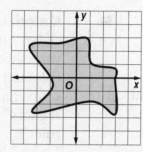

3.

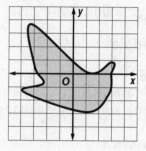

4.   **CHALLENGE**   The figure at the right is a graph of $y = \tan x$.
   a. Estimate the shaded area in terms of units.

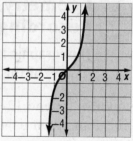

   b. How would your estimate of the shaded area change if you used rectangles with a smaller width?

5.   **WRITING IN MATH**   Describe another method you could use to estimate the area of an irregular figure on the coordinate plane.

Geometry Lab
Recording Sheet

Right Solids and Oblique Solids
(pp. 167–168 of this booklet)

Use With Explore 12-1. This corresponds to the activity on pages 821–822 in the Student Edition.

Objective Identify and draw right and oblique solids. Draw nets.

Materials
none

Students will investigate right and oblique solids by drawing nets.

Answers
See Teacher Edition pp. 821-822.

 Geometry Lab
Recording Sheet

Topographic Maps
(p. 169 of this booklet)

Use with Extend 12-1. This corresponds to the activity on page 829 in the Student Edition.

Objective Interpret and draw topographical maps.

Materials
ruler

Students will read, interpret, and topographical maps.

Answers
See Teacher Edition p. 169.

 Geometry Lab
Surface Areas of Cylinders and Cones
(pp. 170–171 of this booklet)

Use with Lessons 12-2 and 12-3

Objective Find the lateral area and surface area of a right cylinder and a right circular cone.

Materials
classroom set of Geometry Lab worksheets transparency master of Geometry Lab
soup can with label
scissors*
ruler*
* = available in Overhead Manipulative Resources

You may wish to complete the following demonstration before handing out the worksheet.

Demonstration:

Place the transparency master on the overhead. Cover the transparency, revealing only *Figure 1*. Cut a soup can label along a line perpendicular to the base of the can, and remove the label. Lay the paper label flat and identify its area. Have students find the lateral area, $L =$ base $\times$ height, where base $=$ circumference of the can. Use the can to find the total area, $T = L + 2$(area of circle). Uncover Figure 2 on the transparency master and discuss how this relates to the soup can example.

Before students build the cones, ask them how the radius of the sector compares with the slant height of the cone. When students have completed the activity, review the answers with the class.

Answers

1a. $L = 112\pi$, $T = 210\pi$

1b. $L = 240\pi$, $T = 1040\pi$

2a. πr^2

2b. $\dfrac{n}{360}\pi r^2$

2c. $2\pi r$

3. All are 3 cm.

4. A: 6.75π, B: 2.25π, C: 6π, D: 3π

5. The lateral area of cone A is 3 times the lateral area of cone B. The lateral area of cone C is 2 times the lateral area of cone D.

6. ℓ: 3 cm, 3 cm, 3 cm, 3 cm; h: 2 cm, 2.9 cm, 2.3 cm, 2.8 cm; r : 2.25 cm, 0.75 cm, 2 cm, 1 cm

7. See students' work; for each cone in Exercise 6, check that $r^2 + h^2 = \ell^2$.

8. A: 6.75π, B: 2.25π, C: 6π, D: 3π

Mini-Project

Cone Patterns
(p. 172 of this booklet)

Use With Lesson 12-3.

Objective Draw, cut out, and find measurements of cone patterns.

Materials

construction paper
compass*
centimeter ruler*
* = available in Overhead Manipulative Resources

Students can work in groups of two or three for this activity. Using the given measurements, students draw and cut out each cone pattern. For each cone, students find the circumference of the base, height, slant height, lateral area, and surface area.

Answers

1. 5 cm

2. $\dfrac{3}{4}$

3. 31.4 cm

4. 23.56 cm

5. See students' work.

6. 7.5 cm

7. 23.56 cm

8. 5 cm

9. 3.3 cm

10. 58.9 cm^2

11. 103.1 cm^2

12. 8.0 cm; 75.4 cm^2; 4.5 cm

13. 10 cm; 157.1 cm^2; 8.7 cm

Geometry Lab Recording Sheet

Locus and Spheres
(p. 173 of this booklet)

Use With Extend 12-6. This corresponds to the activity on page 872 in the Student Edition.

Objective Find the locus of points a given distance from the end points of a segment.

Materials
straightedge

Students can work in pairs to complete this activity. Students investigate and identify the locus of points that represent a given set of criteria. You may wish to select a student to draw their figure for Exercise 1 on the chalkboard or overhead.

Answers
See Teacher Edition page 872.

Geometry Lab Recording Sheet

Navigational Coordinates
(p. 174 of this booklet)

Use With Extend 12-7. This corresponds to the activity on page 879 in the Student Edition.

Objective Use a latitude and longtitude measure to identify the hemisphere the location lies in and estimate the location of a city using a globe or map.

Materials
globe or map

Students will use latitude and longtitude to locate hemispheres and cities.

Answers
See Teacher Edition page 879.

Mini-Project

Word Search
(p. 175 of this booklet)

Use With Lesson 12-7.

Objective Find and circle each word in the word search. Then find the meaning of each word and a page where it appears in your book.

For this activity, students can work in pairs. Ask students to identify how the meanings they find in a dictionary are different or like the meanings in their Geometry book.

Answers

Geometry Lab Recording Sheet

(Use with Explore 12-1 on pages 821–822 in the Student Edition)

Right Solids and Oblique Solids

Materials: none

Exercises

Identify each figure as a right solid or an oblique solid.

1.

2.

3.

Sketch each solid. Describe the shapes of its bases and late faces.

4. oblique rectangular prism

5. right triangular prism

Teaching Geometry with Manipulatives

Exercises

Draw a net of each figure.

6.

7.

8.

9. *Writing in Math* Explain the difference between a right prism
and an oblique prism.

NAME _____ DATE _____ PERIOD _____

Geometry Lab Recording Sheet

(Use with Extend 12-1 on page 829 in the Student Edition)

Topographic Maps

Materials: ruler

Explore the Model

Use the topographic map to answer these questions.

1. According to the scale, what is the vertical distance between each contour line?

2. What is the difference in height between the lowest and highest points?

3. What do you notice about the contour lines for the peaks of the hills?

4. Describe a steep slope on the topographic map. How do you know it is steep?

5. Explain how you would draw a topographic map given a side view of some hills.

Model and Analyze

6. Draw a possible topographic map similar to the map above for the side view of the hills from points *A* to *B*.

7. Draw a possible side view similar to the map above from points *A* to *B* of the hills from the topographic map. Measures are given in feet.

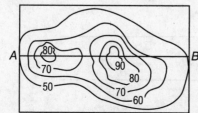

Geometry Lab

(Use with Lessons 12-2 and 12-3)

Surface Areas of Cylinders and Cones

1. Find the lateral area L and surface area S of each right cylinder.

a. $L =$ _____

$S =$ _____

b. $L =$ _____

$S =$ _____

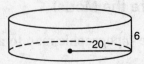

2. List the formulas for each of the following.

a. area of a circle _____

b. area of a sector _____

c. circumference of a circle _____

3. Measure the radius of the sectors on the next page.

A _____ B _____ C _____ D _____

4. Find the lateral area of each sector from Exercise 3.

A _____ B _____ C _____ D _____

5. How do the lateral areas for cones A and B compare? _____

Cones C and D? _____

Construct four cones from the patterns and instructions on the next page.

6. Measure and record the following.

	Cone A	Cone B	Cone B	Cone C
Slant height (*l*)				
height (*h*)				
radius of the base (*r*)				

7. Check the accuracy of your measurements using the Pythagorean Theorem.

Example: $3^2 + 4^2 = 5^2$

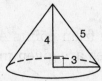

A _____

B _____

C _____

D _____

8. Using the slant height and radius from Exercise 6, find the lateral area of each cone. ($L = \pi r \ell$)

A _____ B _____ C _____ D _____

Steps to Build a Cone

- Cut out the figures below.
- Tape edges (radii) together without overlapping.
- To measure the height of the cone, insert a pencil through the vertex of the cone, mark the length, then measure with a ruler.
- To measure the radius of the base, place the cone on a ruler and measure the widest distance (diameter).

$\left(\text{radius} = \frac{1}{2} \text{ diameter} \right)$

A.

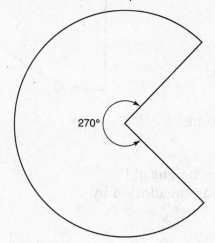

270°

B.

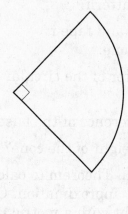

C.

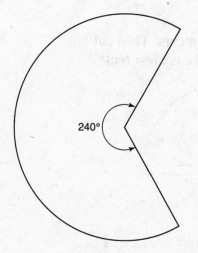

240°

D.

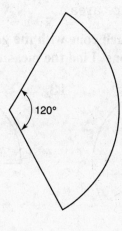

120°

Mini-Project

(Use with Lesson 12-3)

Cone Patterns

Using $AB = 5$ centimeters, draw a pattern shaped like the one at the right. It can be folded to make a cone.

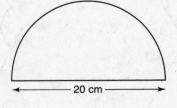

1. Measure the radius of the circle to the nearest centimeter.

2. The pattern is what fraction of the complete circle?

3. What is the circumference of the complete circle?

4. How long is the circular arc that is the outside of the pattern?

5. Cut out the pattern and tape it together to form a cone.

6. Measure the diameter of the circular base of the cone.

7. What is the circumference of the base of the cone?

8. What is the slant height of the cone?

9. Use the Pythagorean Theorem to calculate the height of the cone. Use a decimal approximation. Check your calculation by measuring the height with a metric ruler.

10. Find the lateral area.

11. Find the total surface area.

Make a paper pattern for each cone with the given measurements. Then cut out the pattern and make the cone. Find the measurements to the nearest tenth.

12.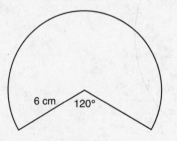

6 cm   120°

13.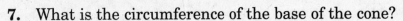

← 20 cm →

diameter of base = _____   diameter of base = _____

lateral area = _____   lateral area = _____

height of cone = _____   height of Cone = _____

Geometry Lab Recording Sheet

(Use with Extend 12-6 on page 872 in the Student Edition)

Locus and Spheres

Materials
straightedge

Analyze

1. Draw a figure and describe the locus of points in space that are 8 units from each endpoint of a given segment that is 30 units long.

2. What three-dimensional shapes from the figure?

3. What are the radii and diameters of each hemisphere?

4. What are the diameter and height of the cylinder?

5. What is the shape of the intersection of the upper hemispheres?

6. Can this be described as a locus of points in space or on a plane? Explain.

7. Describe the intersection as a locus.

8. FIREWORKS What is the locus of points that describe how particles from a firework explosion will disperse in an explosion at ground level if the expected distance a particle could travel is 200 feet?

Geometry Lab Recording Sheet

(Use with Extend 12-7 on page 879 in the Student Edition)

Navigational Coordinates

Materials: map or globe

Activity

1. In which hemisphere is each city located?

City	Latitude	Longitude
A	37° 59′ N	84° 28′ W
B	34° 55′ S	138° 36′ E
C	64° 4′ N	21° 58′ W

2. Use a globe or map to name each city.

3. Earth is approximately a sphere with a radius of 3960 miles. The equator and all meridians are great circles. The circumference of a great circle is equal to the length of the equator or any meridian. Find the length of a great circle on Earth in miles.

4. Notice the distance between each line of latitude is about the same. The distance from the equator to the North Pole is one-fourth the circumference of Earth. So each degree of latitude is one-ninetieth of that distance. Find the approximate distance between one parallel in miles.

Analyze

The table shows the latitude and longitude of three cities.

1. Name the hemisphere where each city is located.

City	Latitude	Longitude
F	1° 28′ S	48° 29′ W
G	13° 45′ N	100° 30′ W
H	41° 17′ S	174° 47′ E

2. Use a globe or map to name of each city.

3. Find the approximate distance between meridians at latitude of about 22° N. The direct distance between the two cities below is about 1646 miles.

Calcutta, India	22° 34′ N	88° 24′ E
Hong Kong, China	22° 20′ N	114° 11′ E

NAME _____ DATE _____ PERIOD _____

Mini-Project

(Use with Lesson 12-7)

Word Search

Each word in the list below can be found in your geometry book. Find and circle each of these words in the word-search puzzle. Then find the meaning of each word in a dictionary, and find a page in your book where each word appears.

AXIS	HYPOTHESIS	PLANES	ROTATION
COLLINEAR	IMAGE	POINT	STATEMENT
COORDINATE	INTERSECT	POSTULATE	SYMMETRY
COUNTEREXAMPLE	NEGATION	PROOF	THEOREM
DIAGONAL	NONCOPLANAR	QUADRANT	TRIANGLE
GRAPH	ORIGIN	REFLECTION	VECTOR

```
A X I D I A G O N A L I E T C S E C N N
P O E R J S O L D F X N I T O R O N N A
C O U N T E R E X A M P L E O O Q M E L
E S T M A N T F E A U N I C R T I A G I
S E O U M U N G E R K O K L D A V S A R
B H C A T M P P Q U A D R A N T N H T E
A O Y O V P V R O R O M F M X I A E I F
H D W P H O Y E U H Q U D R T O N O O R
A E O L O S W S C R K L M E C N T R N E
N O Q V I T E I Y T T O U D O V S E T C
O R S E L U H D F I O N R G L Z N M O T
N C Q O L L O E L I N R S E L E D A M I
C F O P L A N E S I Q L T R I A N G L E
O V O O L T A N R I R D D T N R X A X O
P A C S H E A T P N S R U S E L E S T N
L C S T O C W N O D E N A I A D P T R P
A T T U S S Y R L P C G S M R O A T I R
N O A B J P T I T I H P Y G A M I X J O
A R T H E O R E M S T O M A G L T O I F
R N E D U C A T I A O N M R R R B A N S
P U M U S C I A I L G T E T A K P E G T
O M E B S A V N E N N E T R P C O V T A
I C N L A T M I T R T F R E H O I I L E
N O T I P W A O M E R E Y A R U N D E N
B P I N R G I R O T R F R N E N T M B A
Y L C O O R D I N A T E X S S T Z E E D
P A V L O A V G E D M O S G E E V O N E
O N M X F P T I G O N Q U E S C L S T I
B P Z O G O B N O I R E F L E C T I O N
```

175

Teaching Geometry with Manipulatives

Probability and Measurement
Teaching Notes and Overview

CHAPTER 13

Geometry Lab Recording Sheet

Graph Theory
(pp. 177–178 of this booklet)

Use With Extend 13-6. This corresponds to the activity on pages 946-947 in the Student Edition.

Objective To apply physical models, graphs, and networks to develop solutions in applied contexts.

Materials
none

Students will investigate graph theory using models, graphs, and networks.

Answers
See Teacher Edition pp. 946–947.

Geometry Lab Recording Sheet

(Use with Extend 13-6 on pages 946-947 in the Student Edition)

Graph Theory

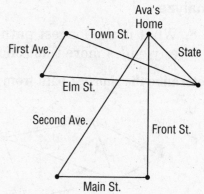

Materials: none

Activity 1

Step 1 Use the graph at the right.

Step 2 Beginning at Ava's home, trace over her route
without lifting your pencil. Remember to trace
each edge only once.

Step 3 Describe Ava's route. Compare your graph with those of your
classmates.

Analyze

1. Is there more than one traceable route that begins at
Ava's house? If so, how many?

2. If it does not matter where Ava starts,
how many traceable routes are possible?

Is each graph is traceable. Write *yes* or *no*. Explain your reasoning.

3. 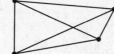   4.    5.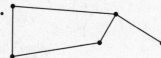

6. The campus for Centerburgh High School has five buildings built
around the edge of a circular courtyard. There is a sidewalk
between each pair of buildings.

   a. Draw a graph of the campus. Is the graph traceable?

   b. Suppose that there is not a sidewalk between the pairs of
   adjacent buildings. Is it possible to reach all five buildings
   without walking down any sidewalk more than once?

7. **REASONING** Write for a rule for determining whether a
graph is traceable.

Analyze

8. What is the longest path from A to B that does not cover any edges more than once?

Determine the shortest path from A to B for each network.

9.

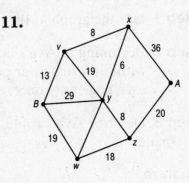

10.

11.

12. **OPEN ENDED** Create your own network with 8 nodes and a shortest path with a value of 25.

13. **WRITING IN MATH** Explain your method for determining the shortest path of a network.

14. **TRAVEL** Use the network below to find each shortest path.

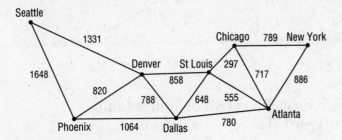

   a. from Phoenix to New York

   b. from Seattle to Atlanta

15. **MOVIES** *Six Degrees of Separation* is a well-known example of graph theory. In this case, each person is a node and people are linked by an edge when they know each other.

   a. Make a graph of the situation. Directly connect yourself to three other people you know personally. This represents the first degree of separation.

   b. Expand the graph to show the first three degrees of separation. Name a person who is within 3 degrees of you and list the path.